Mountains and Hills of Britain

Mountains and Hills of Britain

A Guide to the Uplands of England, Scotland and Wales

Michael Marriott

Foreword by John Hillaby

WILLOW BOOKS
COLLINS
St James's Place London
1982

An Adkinson Parrish Book

Copyright © 1982 by
Adkinson Parrish Limited

Willow Books
William Collins Sons & Co Ltd
London · Glasgow · Sydney
Auckland · Toronto · Johannesburg

First published 1982

British Library Cataloguing in
Publication Data
Marriott, Michael
    Mountains and hills of Britain.
    1. Mountains – Great Britain
    I. Title
    551.4'3'0941 GB542.G/
ISBN 0 00 218028 6

Designed and produced by
Adkinson Parrish Limited, London
Editor   Hilary Dickinson
Art Editor   Christopher White
Designer   Martin Atcherley
Cartographers   Clyde Surveys Ltd

Phototypeset by
Hugh Wilson Typesetting, Norwich

Illustrations originated by
East Anglian Engraving Ltd, Norwich

Printed by Hazell Watson & Viney
Limited, Aylesbury, Bucks

Contents

Foreword

During my first half century on this distracted globe I have been a member of all sorts of curious clubs and societies. Even before I shed my short pants I joined the Leeds Nats, a congregation of dedicated amateur naturalists. With help from gifted all-rounders who could put a name to nearly everything they saw, I explored the Northern moors and fells, walking, note-taking, and collecting plants and insects. Later, lightly disguised as the biological correspondent of an august newspaper, I flew round the world, imperiously, like a trade-union leader. That meant being on nodding terms with professional enquirers at Burlington House in Piccadilly.

I have never really got used to London but, to see it in the round, I went out with the Bug Club, a group of entomologists who met in a pub near Victoria station. A friend who specialized in parasitic wasps invited me to join the first Savage Club and then the Tetrapods who go in for almost anything on four legs from aardvarks to zebras. Now and again I looked in to meetings of the Micros, the classifiers of relatives of the clothes moths, but they were too close to microscopy for my fancy. I preferred the company of robust rock men, the climbers and scramblers who at a glance could explain precisely how our mountains and hills had been freaked into savage beauty by the combined forces of time and subterranean upheavals. Thereafter I became a long-distance walker.

Today it is a little saddening to discover that, although serious walking has become more popular than ever before, only a small proportion of the new generation are recapturing the enquiring spirit of the old naturalists. Perhaps I am being a bit hard on those who are not particularly interested in the strata, the flora and fauna of the countryside, but I have long held that, if you do not know what you are looking at, you cannot be expected to look at it for very long. Witness the reaction of the crowds at the top of a funicular in the Alps. With his affinities with what makes up the world, the field naturalist is able to put a great deal between what he sees and that portion of his mind where boredom lurks. For a competent walker, a knowledge of geology, the build and shape of the land, is as important as a plane table to a surveyor. A good amateur should be able to determine what is underfoot as readily as a person who likes cheeses can immediately distinguish between hard parmesan, crumbling cheshire, viscous camembert, variable cheddar, and rubbery edam.

For example, anyone who has walked the Pennine Way knows that in the vicinity of Lothersdale the harsh feel of the millstone grit is replaced by the springy turf that clothes its geological bed-fellow, the carboniferous limestone, and the flora is entirely different. Likewise, the reassuring grip of the gabbro in the Cuillins of Skye is rendered dangerous by intrusions of basalt which are slippery, especially after rain. If your feet are not in good condition it is unwise to tackle the hard Cambrian grits of the Rhinogs of North Wales. And, like the formations on the Isle of Skye, some of the rocks thereabouts are ferromagnetic, so watch your compass.

We live in an age when the popular heroes of our culture are mostly TV stars, pop singers, and the outstanding figures of organized sport. Fortunately, the success of David Attenborough's programmes show there is enormous sympathy with those able to explain the component parts of the world we live in. Such people used to be called all-round naturalists. Nowadays the specialists are known as ecologists. The word means neither more nor less than the study of the home of things, the way in which organisms live in relationship to each other, and the soil to which they are attached.

Those who explore mountains and hills are members of an élite. There is the physical difficulty in getting up there and the satisfaction in knowing they are exploring a whole range of habitats populated for the most part by specialized plants and animals. One of the pioneers was Thomas Johnson, that great botanist who lived in troubled times and died, eventually, of his wounds as a Cavalier soldier. His account of the ascent of Snowdon in 1639 is one all walkers and naturalists will enjoy, especially perhaps the concluding sentences: 'Leaving our horses and outer garments, we began to climb the mountain. The ascent at first is difficult but, after a bit, broad open space is found, but equally sloping, great precipices on the left and a difficult climb on the right. Having climbed three miles, we at last gained the highest ridge of the mountain which was shrouded in thick cloud. Here the way was very narrow, and climbers are horror-stricken by the rough, rocky precipices on either hand, and the Stygian marshes, both on this side and that. We sat down in the midst of the clouds, and first of all arranged in order the plants we had, at our peril, collected among the rocks and precipices, and then we ate the food we had brought with us.'

Note the priorities. Homer could not have put it better. Michael Marriott is an experienced traveller. His earth scans have taken him from Africa to the outbacks of Australia by way of Afghanistan. In this wide-ranging and gloriously illustrated book, his knowledge is focused on the eminences of these islands of ours which, among many reasons, are unique in that we have examples of all known geological systems. Mr Marriott will be the first to admit that, to carry out a project of this scope completely, would require a shelf of books far thicker than this one. I disagree with some of the things he has to say, but then I am quite sure that, in a spirit of scientific dissatisfaction, he would disagree with some of mine. That is what natural history is all about.

Mountaineering is a skill, long-distance walking is a fine art, biology and geology are sciences. To study them in the great outdoors is often a science, an art frequently but, for the studious amateur, play for most of the time. And who shall stop the British at their honest play?

John Hillaby

Introduction

The mountains and hills of the British Isles form one of the finest outdoor leisure grounds in the western world. Whatever the aspirations of the high-country enthusiast – whether to indulge in the gentlest of footpath strolls, or to train for a climbing assault on Everest – there is a splendid variety of terrain to suit personal levels of energy output and physical ambition.

From the heady heights of the Lake District to the voluptuous rounded contours of the South Downs, these uplands are almost the last remaining open country where the city-dweller can stretch the body and uplift the spirit. The mountains and hills of western Europe in general, and of Great Britain in particular, have never been so much appreciated as they are today. For the hills have a timeless, magnetic appeal and to roam them freely on foot is a priceless privilege appreciated by an ever-increasing number of people. In the pages that follow I hope to illuminate the high country a little more for those who already feel an affinity, who want to draw somewhat closer than the beauty-spot car park or designated picnic area.

Since Sir Edward Whymper first stood on the summit of the Matterhorn in 1865, the Swiss Alps and their counterparts the world over have been viewed as a sporting challenge by the climbing fraternity. Technical climbing, however, is highly specialized with its own mystique, literature, and language, and this area has been largely omitted in the interest of a wider, less-experienced readership, although all recognized climbing areas in the British Isles are pinpointed. Purist climbing is scarcely the province of the novice and so the line is drawn at modest rock-scrambling, the natural follow-up to hill-walking which may be enjoyed safely with no special hardware, costly equipment, or high level of expertise.

Britain is a land of hills rather than mountains. We do have a scattering of giants like Scafell Pike, Snowdon, Ben Nevis, and others like Cader Idris, Ben Cruachan, and the Cairn Gorm. In the main, though, our high country is less immediately dramatic, seldom exceeding 3000 feet of elevation.

Britain's acknowledged mountains are located in tight-knit clusters and the land-mass covered collectively by the Lake District, the Cuillins, Snowdonia, the Cairngorms, and elsewhere, really is very small indeed. It is therefore even more remarkable that within its compass the landscape is so widely different. And if mountains are in somewhat short supply, no country of comparable size is so blessed with hill ranges so distinctly contrasting in make-up and character.

Prospects for the aspiring wanderer today could hardly be brighter. Most of the high ground is preserved as National Park, or is zealously protected by the National Trust. Access is now justly free to all. Most, if not all, the important footpaths are waymarked and there is extensive literature and specialized maps covering all long-distance routes like the Pennine Way and Offa's Dyke Path. (The relevant Ordnance Survey maps (1 : 50000 series) are listed at the end of each chapter in this book.) For the visitor with climbing aspirations, preferring direct elevation rather than hill-top traversing, there is a large number of guide books on areas like the Lake District or Snowdonia. A list of further reading for beginners is provided at the end of this book.

Wherever you live in the British Isles, the uplands are never far distant. Scotland and Wales, the west and north of England are rich in hill country; in the centre and the south lie the Cotswolds, the Chilterns, the North and South Downs, while much of the coast itself is girded with cliffs. Even East Anglia, more renowned for watery Broadlands, boasts a swathe of attractive high country around Sheringham, Norfolk.

It should therefore not be difficult to instigate a routine of healthy self-improvement which costs little, other than leisure time, returns much, and can be as casual as you wish. It may be that you never feel the need to graduate from gentle strolling in the hills at week-ends or holidays. No

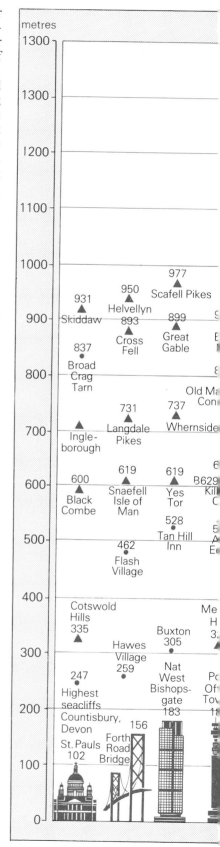

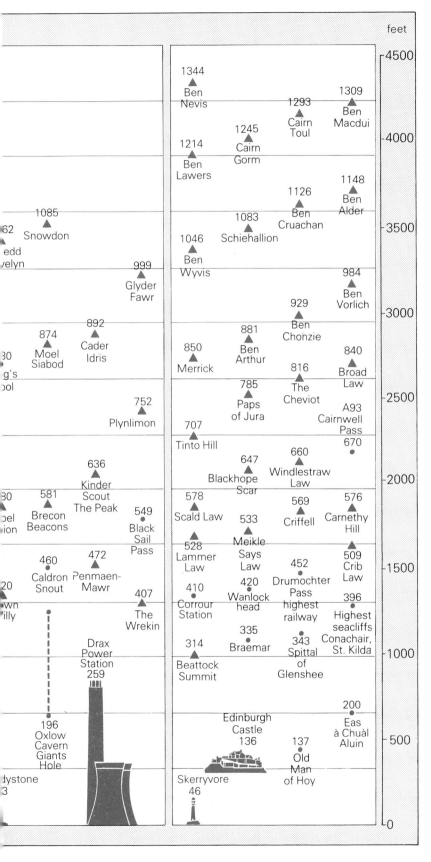

Left Diagram of comparative heights of the main hills and mountains in the British Isles.

9

Above A group of walkers enjoying an exhilarating view over the Snowdonian ridges from their high vantage-point.

Below The majestic line of peaks which greet the eye on the approach to Wasdale in the Lake District National Park. Great Gable rises in the centre.

matter. Conversely – and this is what I hope to spark – you might find yourself embarking on a love-affair with the high country that will grow in intensity and last for a lifetime.

Nothing spurs dedication more than a challenging, if distant, objective. After a trial walk or two in your home hills, it may be that an ascent of Snowdon or a traverse of the North Yorks Moors becomes an increasingly alluring prospect. As you gain in confidence and stamina, such a venture may become a distinctly practical proposition.

Hasten slowly, though, and learn the rudiments before taking too deep a plunge. While experience builds confidence, there are many things which go to make the expert high-country enthusiast. The climber must be a good hill-walker, since it is often necessary to trek to chosen rock faces; the good hill-walker should be able to cope with elementary rock-scrambling in case the need arises. Scrambling, by the way, may be loosely defined as ascending or descending scarps or scree slopes using the hands occasionally, but never ropes or climbing hardware.

All those who aspire to high-country pursuits should be able to read map and compass properly and to interpret the information contained in Ordnance Survey maps. A basic knowledge of first-aid is also to be recommended; it may only be used once but may prove vital to survival should the worst ever happen. It also helps to know how to extract the best from the human machine. It is sound common sense to limit energy output to capability. You should pace yourself like a boxer or runner, recognizing danger signs like over-tiredness and correcting them by eating quick-energy food, and being able to detect the insidious onset of hypothermia and take the appropriate evasive measures. (See Safety First, p.164.)

Anyone who has tramped even the gentlest of foothills knows how deceptive distances are. If there is one rule that the potential foot-traveller should remember to keep clear of trouble, it is that tried and trusted formula which decrees that one hour be allowed for every three miles on the map,

plus one hour more for every 2000 feet of altitude. It is worth remembering, too, that climatically, 3000 feet of elevation in Britain is equal to 8000 feet on the Continent.

Weather lore can be learned, to an extent, by home study, but many of the dodges that make moving about the mountains safe, smooth, and easy have to be learned in the field. Keeping on the same contour line, where possible, around a mountain conserves energy; wandering up and down erratically wastes it. Crossing a swollen stream barefoot is far better than boulder-hopping at the risk of a bootful of water, particularly early in the day.

You can go it alone in glorious isolation, or you can learn the rudiments of the Mountain Game in the company of others. The British Mountaineering Council exists to foster the interests of climbers and hill-walkers and is recognized by The Sports Council. All users of the mountains are entitled to look to the BMC for authoritative help, although members are largely concerned with the sport of mountaineering. Among the many excellent publications which the BMC distributes is a nationwide list of centres which run courses in mountaineering and allied activities. A selection will be found at the end of this book (pp.166–9).

Enthusiasm being best imparted by example, much of the body of this book is devoted to the practical aspects of upland discovery: suitable approach routes; degrees of difficulty; convenient base camps; car parks; natural or man-made gems in the vicinity and any other factor which may be useful in the field, or add interest to each excursion.

Possibly some new high country may be revealed to the reader who has not been able to travel these islands as extensively as I have been fortunate to do, both for pleasure and in the course of duty. A fair proportion of the terrain included is not necessarily the best known or the most visited. Nor need it be, since this is something of a personal choice of high country savoured – and deeply enjoyed – throughout twenty-five years of what might be termed purposeful hill-wandering.

Above The Wye Valley above Hay-on-Wye, from the Black Mountains.

Left Walkers near Great End, overlooking the Langdales, one of the most popular walking and climbing areas in Lakeland.

Geology

For the most part, the British Isles are densely populated and have endured a long history of urban and industrial development. But, despite the ravages that have been wrought on these tiny islands by housing, mining, road-building, and modern mechanized farming, they remain essentially green and pleasant. Indeed, in Britain, the pedestrian traveller is able to encounter a richer variety of scenery during the course of a single day than in almost any other part of the world. The foundation upon which Britain's landscape tapestry is laid is the bed-rock beneath, and the geology of these islands is as complex and varied as the scenery it supports.

Over the last ten or twenty years, great advances have been made in the understanding of the way in which our planet, Earth, has evolved and continues to change its face. All is not quite what it seems, and the Earth is not just the solid sphere that it may appear to be. Here is

not the place to dwell upon the physics of our planet but it is worth considering for a moment the way in which it is constructed so that we may appreciate all the more the wonders of the landscape. Briefly, the Earth may be compared to an onion in the shape of a flattened ball. It is made up in layered fashion with a solid central core, a liquid outer core, surrounding which is the mantle in a kind of semi-plastic state. On this mantle floats the thin outer skin on which we walk – the crust. But even this crust is not all of a piece; most geologists today believe that it can be thought of as a three-dimensional spherical jigsaw made up of rigid plates of crust which move over the aeons of time in relation to one another. Perhaps they may be driven in near-perpetual motion by currents within the mobile mantle. As these plates move about the globe, they may crash into each other, one may disappear beneath another, or new crust

may be formed between them as near-liquid basalt rock is spewed up between two plates, forcing them apart. As this motion continues relentlessly over the millennia, rocks bend and break, oceans are created and destroyed, mountain ranges are thrown up only to be torn down again by raging winds and driving rain, and layer upon layer of new rocks to be are laid down as sediments on the ocean floors. It is a world of continuous change but, during our meagre life-span of three score and ten, we notice little difference because the Earth has had some 4500 million years to put on its latest face!

By an accident of geological chance, Britain has been caught up in the turmoil of the Earth more than most, so that a cursory glance at the *Geological Map of the British Islands* published by the Ordnance Survey will quickly reveal the many different kinds of rock that outcrop as well as the variety and complexity of

PRE-CAMBRIAN ERA
up to 570 million years ago*

570–225 PALAEOZOIC ERA

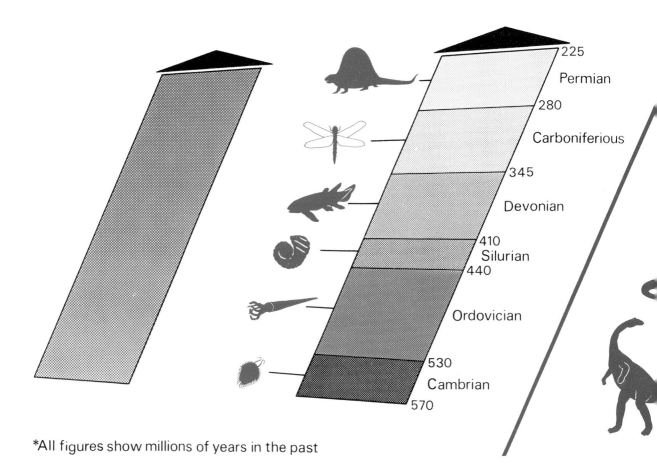

225
Permian
280
Carboniferous
345
Devonian
410
Silurian
440
Ordovician
530
Cambrian
570

*All figures show millions of years in the past

12

their structure. Perhaps this is one of the main reasons why the British Isles have, in the main, been the cradle of geology.

There are three main kinds of rocks. Those which have welled up from the depths either as semi-molten masses, such as the granites of Dartmoor and the south-west, or as more fluid basalts, such as those of Anglesey, are known as igneous rocks. Those which have resulted from the compaction and uplifting of rock detritus laid down at the bottom of a lake or ocean, or forming the wind-blown sediments of an ancient desert, are sedimentary rocks. Finally, there are rocks that have been formed from existing materials which have been subjected to intense heat and pressure during the bubbling-up of a granite or the making of a mountain chain. These are referred to as metamorphic or 'changed' rocks and include the glittering mica-rich schists with their studs or garnets and the hard, often ancient gneisses that can be seen in

the north-west of Scotland.

To bring order out of chaos, early geologists divided the time span of Earth's history, represented by the record of the rocks, into various eras, periods, and epochs. Fossils are the preserved remains in the rocks of ancient life forms and these help us to unravel the mysteries of the 'geological clock' because different kinds of animals have lived at different periods of the Earth's evolution. It was once thought that there were no animals or plants living earlier than about 600 million years ago so that the 4000 million years which went before were called the Azoic, or period with no life. The span of time following was then divided into major eras, the Paleozoic (ancient life), the Mesozoic (middle life), and the Cainozoic (recent life). These, in turn, are further divided into periods which, from the oldest to the youngest, are as follows: the Cambrian, Ordovician, Silurian, Devonian, Car-

boniferous, Permian, Triassic, Jurassic, Cretaceous, Tertiary, and Quaternary. The reasons for the names of some of the periods can be guessed. For example, Cambria was an early name for Wales where rocks of this age were first described whereas Ordovices and Silures were ancient Welsh tribes. The Carboniferous, too, spanning a period from about 350 million years ago to 280 million years, is the age in which most of the deposits were laid down that have given rise to the coal upon which we still depend for energy.

All of these different groups of rocks, with their different physical characteristics, and subjected to variations in climate as well as the many periods of upheaval throughout time, form the basis for the wonderful diversity of

Below Chart showing the main evolutionary eras.

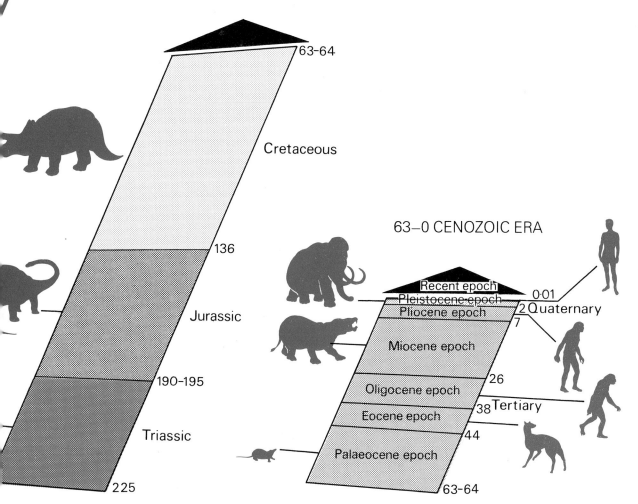

countryside for which Britain is justly
famed. The walker crossing the bleak
expanses of Dartmoor is treading on an
igneous rock that forced its way upwards
through younger sediments some 280
million years ago and is now gradually
being worn away as the crumbling tors
surrounded by the tumbled 'clitters'
readily reveal. Around the south-west
peninsula it is possible to traverse
Devonian sandstones, Carboniferous
grits and coals, ancient igneous rocks of
various kinds such as the serpentinite of
the Cornish Lizard Peninsula, or fossil-
rich, Jurassic clays, marls, and lime-
stones of Dorset. In the latter it is even
possible to see the footprints of a long-
dead dinosaur! The western section of
the Ridgeway largely follows the line of
a ridge of Cretaceous chalk that represents the remains of countless millions
of tiny animals and plants that were
deposited at the bottom of shallow seas
perhaps bordering a desert area; likewise
much of the South and North Downs.
Further north, the fell-walker in the Lake
District may stride across magnificent
hills composed of three main divisions of
rocks: the Skiddaw Slates, the Borrowdale Volcanics and the Silurian Slates
and Flags each of which has been subjected to a different style of folding so
that, even within an area as tiny as the
Lakes, which may seem to be relatively
uniform, there are local differences which
are heightened by the activities of the
glaciers of the Ice Ages.

Further north still, the Highlands and
islands of Scotland are, for many
hardened or not so hardened walkers,
the Mecca of Britain. Here are some of
the oldest rocks to be found in Britain
such as the Torridonian sandstones and
Lewisian gneisses of the far north-west
among which it is still possible to be 'far
from the madding crowd'.

Right Drag fold, associated with an
overthrust. Saundersfoot beach, Dyfed.

Prehistory

The prehistoric period of Britain is represented by mysterious Stonehenge; countless other stone circles; long barrows and Iron Age forts. While the study of these artefacts is not obligatory to enjoyment, it does add fascinating dimensions. The British Isles may be small in area, but no land is richer in relics of Man's early existence.

Signs of Man's activity since his early evolution are particularly evident amid high country, where the landscape is relatively untouched by progress. Here in the uplands are to be found most of the remnants of settlements which were built high up for practical, tactical, or religious reasons. From such evidence we can learn not only about the settlements themselves, but also about the kind of people that lived in them.

The Ancient Briton, for example, far from being the primitive savage of popular conception, is now credited by anthropologists as being not so very different from ourselves. Smaller in stature and preoccupied with survival certainly, but scarcely the aimless, woad-daubed creature so long depicted.

This proof of higher intellect and industry than was previously, and rather imperiously, assumed, is provided by carbon-dating and other sophisticated techniques. Doing your own detective work about early Britons is as rewarding a pastime as is geology in revealing the earth's origins. It illustrates how important the high country was to early Man – as it is today – though of course for vastly different reasons.

Intriguing clues to a past age of quite organized existence are provided by, for instance, that enigmatic figure, Wilmington Long Man. Carved into the chalk of a Sussex hillside near Eastbourne, this giant outline of a human figure holding a staff in each hand was for long thought to have been cut in the Middle Ages. It is now conjectured that the figure is far older, conceivably early Saxon or Viking. King Harold is one suggested candidate, though the real age simply is not known. It is the staffs held by the figure that have aroused curiosity in learned circles. The assumption that they are vestigial kingly accoutrements, spears or shepherd's crooks, has been questioned in favour of a more acceptable theory. The Long Man is a high priest of ancient society, a surveyor. What he actually holds with those outstretched arms are surveying poles. When this is propounded the hypothesis becomes one of some substance.

Above The stone circle at Castlerigg, near Keswick in Cumbria, is one of many sites of pagan worship to be found in the British uplands.

Right Mystery surrounds the age and identity of the figure of the Long Man, carved into the chalk at Wilmington, East Sussex.

Many of Britain's hill-tracks and green roads have been in existence for around 3000 years, and probably a great deal longer. They were the first communication routes established when the land was largely one of uncharted, dangerous swamps and impenetrable forests, routes that were crucial to transport vital commodities like salt which was more precious than gold during the Stone, Bronze, and Iron Ages.

It is therefore understandable that anyone who could engineer direct access over high ground to such a treasured resource should be held in exhalted esteem in ancient society. With two poles and basic geometry, those early surveyors laid tracks direct to distant, fruitful horizons. The evidence of the strange Ley Lines also shows that some highly intelligent brains were at work at the very dawn of history, even if today we cannot fathom their precise purpose.

Was the Long Man of Wilmington one such wizard? At any event, those with an enquiring mind walking the South Downs in the vicinity of Alfriston have cause to give this particular chalk-cut figure something more than a passing glance. Equally fascinating are the scattered standing stones of Arbor Low, in the Peak District National Park, calculated to be 4000 years old and ranking in importance with Stonehenge

and Avebury. Who were the people who erected this once-massive temple in such a desolate spot? There are more questions than answers at present to many of Britain's most ancient remains.

Prehistoric man, at first struggling desperately for food and protection against elements and enemies, left little evidence of his existence, crude flint implements apart, since he was essentially a nomad. Not until he progressed to be a grower of food was stability and more permanent habitation possible.

Eventually, time for contemplation gave birth to higher thought, speculation about existence, and the emergence of religion. Pagan worship followed by conversion to Christianity, and war, were the two primary concerns of ancient tribes, once the basic needs of life were satisfied. It is these two factors that are responsible for the majority of prehistoric remains in these islands, especially in the uplands.

Not only was high ground strategic, it was also nearest to Heaven. At any event, the Britain of today is blessed with a wealth of tangible clues to times past. Investigation of every era, from the Stone Age to Medieval times, can uncover much that may appear dull yet is highly revealing about our heritage. A number of examples will be touched upon in the ensuing chapters.

Vegetation and Landscape

When Man first inhabited these islands, they were almost entirely covered by dense forest. Like all living things, however, the surface of the landscape is constantly, if imperceptibly, changing. It is affected subtly by climatic or geological causes, drastically and often alarmingly by Man.

Today there remain no more than a few pockets of the once-dominant broadleaved forests; the clearance was begun by Ancient Britons, and in many places the landscape changed beyond all recognition with the arrival of the bulldozer and agricultural technology. Exploitation, springing from consumer expectations and the need to feed a teeming population, has resulted in the transformation of vast tracts of East Anglia, while half the woodland trees of Britain are now conifers, only three species of which are native. Commerical afforestation has changed the scene in the Borders to one more akin to Canada.

Despite – or perhaps because of – intensive tree-planting, factory-farming on a scale inconceivable to our forefathers, and the horrific advance of concrete, there is now an almost grim determination to protect and preserve what remains of our rural heritage. It is heartening to every ecologist that we still manage to retain vestiges of the pastoral life that obtained before the Industrial Revolution.

To take just one example: notwithstanding widespread and often ill-conceived grubbing of precious hedgerows, there are still some 500 000 miles intact, enclosing farm fields, lining lanes and tracks, and providing home for a whole variety of flora and fauna. Some hedges – Saxon boundary markers in particular – have been in existence for a thousand years. Hedgerows are still one of the most prominent features of Britain's landscape then, the total area of hedging approaching a staggering 450 000 acres. Although under constant threat, they are now recognized as a priceless asset. For the pedestrian traveller, the small, fascinating world of the hedgerow is nearly always close at hand in Britain, a source of endless pleasure to the naturalist. Roughly three-quarters of all indigenous plant species of the British Isles can be found along hedgerows and banks, especially those where traffic is mainly pedestrian.

Grass is the most prominent farm crop in Great Britain, and the variety of wild flowers found on natural grassland is bewildering in its variety. Those walking the Ridgeway Path in Wiltshire in spring can study a host of wild flowers, almost literally beneath the feet, where great sweeps of sweet grasses stretch away to either side of the ancient track.

The seemingly bare hills of the high moorland are graced by heathers, glorious in bloom, accentuating the beauty of the scattered Foxglove; while on the rocky slopes of the wilder coastline the Juniper shrub and Sea Holly cling tenaciously to their wind-swept habitat. In total contrast, the most luxuriant examples of British botanical life are to be found in areas like the heavily wooded Wye Valley and the steep, sheltered combes of Devonshire.

It is a green and pleasant landscape, its scenery as richly varied as is its geological composition. No island in the world contains such contrasting aspects within such a small compass, and this applies notably to the uplands. From the pastoral, almost park-like, gentleness of the Home Counties hills, to the savage grandeur of the Cairngorms; from the clean-cut cliffs of Dorset to the splintered cragginess of the western Highlands, there is enough scenic variety to last the explorer several lifetimes.

Explore and enjoy then, but before turning to the hills take time to consider not only self-preservation (see Safety First, p.164), but also preservation of the countryside you intend visiting. While it should not be necessary to emphasize that we are visitors and not invaders, it is not everyone who cares deeply – or indeed cares at all – about our green spaces.

Regrettably, in an age when remote mountain-rescue telephones are vandalized, dry-stone walls deliberately toppled, and fragile wonders like Osprey nests mindlessly smashed, it is doubly vital that the majority of us behave in a caring way. After all, it is *our* land, and it seems almost superfluous to suggest that we should treasure that which we love.

The fact that this reminder is necessary simply confirms that there is a worm within our species. We must guard against transgression in the countryside, even if inadvertent. The ecology of the British Isles is delicately balanced. It is a priceless heritage, too, that should command the stoutest, most sustained defence. Thoughtless behaviour is little better than deliberate vandalism. So please follow the Country Code, see the countryside as keeper not poacher, and among the hills and mountains take only photographs, leave only footprints.

Left Thrift (*Armeria maritima*), also known as Sea-pink, is common round the coasts of Britain.

Natural History

Despite the dwindling number of habitats, the British Isles are still rich in wildlife. The total population of mammals, birds, reptiles, and amphibians (including migrants) is in excess of 500 species. Specialist observers apart, no one is more likely to share this wonderful world of nature than the wanderer amid the quiet hills, mountains, or coastal cliffs.

Wildlife parks, zoos, and bird sanctuaries provide artificial havens, but there is nothing to compare with the thrill of coming upon a truly wild creature in its natural surroundings. Those who have ever experienced the stunning good fortune to see a badger or non-urban fox going unsuspecting about its business will know the exciting and lasting joy that such a confrontation brings. Man, a great enemy of wild creatures, is avoided if possible, so it is only those humans who tread quietly and circumspectly who will enjoy the wondrous wealth of wildlife that does still abound.

Mammals

Britain is home for some 60 species of mammals, ranging from the monarch of the high mountains, the gentle, vegetarian Red Deer, to the tiny and voracious Common Shrew which eats its own weight in insects daily. In between there are the Grey Seals that colonize our rocky shores in autumn; to the ubiquitous Hedgehog to be seen rooting in almost any hedgerow, outside the hibernation season.

Downland is the habitat of the Brown Hare, a delight to watch, especially in early spring when it performs its madcap courtship dances. To see his rarer cousin, the Blue Hare (whose coat turns white in winter), one must roam the high mountain-tops. Within woodland depths, the timid Fallow Deer – master of camouflage – is the visual reward of the stealthy, sharp-eyed walker.

Those following rivers or walking by lake or coast in some parts of the country may be lucky, and privileged, enough to spot the shy and largely nocturnal Otter, the bright-eyed comedian of the animal world, totally enchanting to watch when indulging in those incredible agile acrobatics. The home of Britain's rarest mammal, the Pine Marten, is now confined to the deep and secret recesses of the Highlands and to Ireland and parts of North Wales, where the conifer forests are thickest. The almost equally rare Wild Cat, tabby in appearance, untameably tigerish by nature, shares the same

hunting-ground. Only the most adventurous walker is likely to catch a glimpse of these handsome carnivores, which were so long mercilessly hunted by man.

In the wooded hills of Wales, the Polecat (with its old name Foulmart on account of the musky scent) lives largely on a diet of Rabbits, while its smaller cousins the Stoat and the Weasel are much more widely distributed and more common than might be thought; a tribute to their efficiency as hunters. Almost as common as the humble Rabbit (brought to Britain by the Normans), is the Grey Squirrel introduced from America in the latter part of the nineteenth century. Our native Red Squirrel has declined in numbers as the Grey Squirrel has spread and now clings desperately to small areas, mainly in the Highlands, Ireland, the Lake District, and the West Country.

Birds

Including migrant visitors, there are over 450 species of birds in Britain, many if not most of which may be spotted by the knowledgeable observer walking our diverse island terrain. The more rugged sea-cliffs, notably those along the western seaboard, make an attractive if uneasy resting place for a number of beautiful sea-birds, such as the Fulmar, Guillemot, Shag, and Great Black-backed Gull. To witness their graceful flight is reason enough to walk the wilder cliffs.

The freshwater and coastal margins contain countless waders, and these together with the largest British wader, the Curlew, may be found nesting on moorland during the summer. With a unique and haunting cry, this elegant bird reflects all that is evocative of the wild and emptier places.

Those tramping in woodland always have the chance of seeing the exotic Greater-spotted Woodpecker; the Long-eared Owl; the colourful little Cross-bill, busy extracting seeds from conifer cones.

Far left The Red Deer, one of the most majestic of British mammals, is now confined mainly to high mountain areas.

Left The Fox is one species that has adapted itself to live with man and is now found in the London suburbs as well as in the countryside.

It is among the high peaks of the far North that our largest bird of prey may be seen, the kingly Golden Eagle. This powerful and magnificent winged hunter will be found only in the most inaccessible of mountain fastnesses.

Reptiles and amphibians

Three species of snakes and three of lizards comprise the total reptile population of Britain; only the Adder is poisonous and will only strike if provoked. Its home is among dry heath, moorland, and cliffs and, like all cold-blooded vertebrates, it hibernates in winter.

The Grass Snake (rare in Scotland) grows up to 3 feet in length and likes open woods, ditches, and water margins. The Smooth Snake is the rarest species; it is now fully protected and lives largely around the Hampshire New Forest. The Slow Worm, which is a legless lizard, lives a burrowing life amid woodland borders and embankments. The Sand Lizard is another rarity, while the Common Lizard is common and widespread.

Among British amphibians, the Natter-jack Toad still survives (just), but is extremely rare, unlike the Common Toad which is widely distributed. The rough skin and smaller size make the toad easily distinguishable from the Common Frog which is smoother. The Great Crested Newt is the largest amphibian, growing to some 6 inches or more in length, the Smooth Newt the commonest and most widespread, but not among mountains. If you see one in the high country it is almost certainly a Palmate Newt, the smallest species, a devotee of peat pools among the peaks; when fully grown it is about 3 inches in length.

Animals without backbones

Midges, mosquitoes, and horse-flies are sworn enemies of most hill-wanderers, but fortunately they form only a fraction of the insect world, which is fascinating to most nature lovers, totally engrossing to some. Insects belong to the near-countless group of invertebrates known as arthropods, which also includes other groups, that share the common feature of having jointed legs, such as spiders, woodlice, mites, centipedes, and so on.

The favourite and most visually attractive insects to the casual observer are the butterflies. Rarest and most handsome is the Swallowtail; most common, the Large White. The Red Admiral and the Peacock are among the brightest and most commonly confused. Nothing epitomizes the lazy days of high summer than the glimpse of bright, delicate wings which flash for so brief a life.

21

Weather Lore

Every excursion to the hills can, and should, be a voyage of discovery, a fulfilling enjoyment of an environment always rich in visual delight, occasionally bestowing moments of pure magic. It does not matter whether it is among the gentle Chilterns or the jagged Cuillins, if the mood of achievement is right.

The variety of hill country within the British Isles is so wide that some form of reward invariably awaits over the next hill-top or mountain summit. Expanding knowledge of this Great Outdoors through self-education often results in the Compleat Countryman, albeit one of amateur status. This includes learning about the upland climate, where it is possible to experience four seasons in a single day.

Cynics claim that while other countries enjoy climates, Britain merely has weather. Our islands are often called wind-swept and sodden, but this is only partly true. Rainy days per annum do average 175 in the lowlands and from 200 to 250 among hills and mountains; this may seem high, but compared with global figures the rain is neither heavy nor prolonged. In Bombay, for example, the average annual rainfall is 71 inches. In England and Wales it is half this total.

In point of fact, Great Britain enjoys a genuinely temperate climate with a temperature that only fluctuates gently whatever the season. Extremes are generally the lot of other lands. Average winter temperatures usually range between 32° and 45°F; in summer, they vary between 55° and 73°F. Extremes of temperature can occur throughout the total time scale, but the modest 10 degrees of variation between upper winter and lower summer temperatures is the benign norm.

This is comforting knowledge for all those who would take to the hills, though it should never make for complacency, since even our comparatively gentle climate can veer swiftly from capricious to fatal in rugged high country. It pays to develop a shrewd weather-eye.

Cloud interpretation is one obvious aspect. Many people may know that when a blue sky is intermingled with green at sunset, rain is likely. The more knowledgeable will be less concerned about this coloration (usually heralding showers) than about a yellow sunset. This is one of the more depressing signs, since it is often the harbinger of gales and heavy, prolonged rain. Such intelligence can be helpful to anyone tramping a stern section of the Pennine Way, for

instance. It can help him decide whether to pitch a pup tent, or seek more solid shelter for the night.

It is also helpful to know that rain belts accompanying depressions usually last for about four hours, and that the slower the cloud build-up, the longer the precipitation will be. In high country, this may not only be rain, but snow, sleet, or hail, accompanied by high winds and a resulting steep fall in temperature.

One indication of bad weather is when the cotton-wool cumulus clouds grow dramatically in size, then turn into the heavy, dense mass known as cumulo-nimbus. Subsequent rainfall is then almost inevitable. High, slow-moving wisps of cirrus, or cirrostratus clouds, can generally be taken as a sign of settled weather, especially in summer.

Fog, or the more frequent mountain mist, is one of the least pleasant weather hazards. In early morning the peaks may often be shrouded in mist. Always wait patiently for clearance and adhere to the recognized safety procedure: 'if in doubt, do nowt'. At night, when a clear moon is ringed, or becomes gradually blurred, this frequently heralds the advance of a front and unsettled weather; a clue to conditions likely to prevail for any trek on the following day.

To be caught in the open during a sudden summer thunderstorm can be nerve-racking. Take comfort from the fact that statistically the chances of being struck by lightning are something like a million to one. Lessen the odds even more by steering yourself away from isolated hill or mountain peaks (where lightning does often strike twice), and tall, solitary trees. Do not hold steel objects and keep a low profile when the storm is raging immediately overhead, preferably away from open spaces, in the shelter of rocks or a stone wall.

Learn as much as you can about the weather then, but never rely entirely on your own interpretation. Before any projected assault on the high country, especially where elevation is in excess of 2000 feet, always seek the reassurance of more scientific sources. Local weather forecasts are obtainable from adventure centres and National Park information offices, and The Meteorological Office publishes an excellent leaflet, 'Weather Advice to the Community'.

Right Cloud interpretation is one important aspect of weather lore. Dense cumulus clouds usually indicate bad weather.

First Steps

Britain boasts more than 100 000 miles of designated footpaths. The bulk of this huge total criss-crosses hill country of one kind or another, either hinterland or coastal. The British Mountaineering Council estimates that the high country of these islands is tramped by some 500 000 hill-walkers, while the mountains and recognized rock-climbing areas are tackled by about 45 000 climbers.

It follows, therefore, that despite the massive total mileage the paths on the fells and elsewhere must be fairly hard pressed at times. Climbers too are becoming increasingly concerned about pressure on their leisure grounds where, in some popular spots, like the gritstone edges of the Peak District or the vicinity of Llanberis Pass in Snowdonia, enthusiasts sometimes literally queue to climb.

This situation, rightly worrying to environmentalists and exasperating to experienced hill-walkers and climbers, can be something of a comfort to the tyro; at least initially. For he, or she, will never be stranded in isolation no matter how seemingly remote the location. In the summer months at least, provided you are on an established footpath you will not be alone for long. Later, as an experienced graduate, you can penetrate the secret high country which still – happily – exists in a number of pockets.

This knowledge should help to bolster confidence when the landscape becomes stern, the elements hostile, and you feel distinctly vulnerable. For the right mental attitude is every bit as important as the clothes and equipment needed for serious high-country exploration. None the less, clothing and equipping oneself efficiently does play a major part in every successful high-country venture, and should be done with due care and consideration.

Footwear

The feet are obviously of prime importance to anyone eager to swap city streets for hill-paths. And since the car or bus-stop will not always be just around the corner (or those paths always be springy, sheep-cropped turf), it pays to ensure that foot comfort has a high priority. All of us who walk for pleasure nowadays owe thanks to one Vitale Bramani, who in the early fifties invented and perfected the Vibram boot sole, now almost a generic term among hill-walkers and climbers.

It is a composite material of extreme toughness which ensures reasonable light weight, gives a sure grip on most surfaces encountered in the hills, and, by virtue of the pattern, almost 'self-sheds' glutinous mud. Cleated to natural leather uppers and shanked with a hickory inset to prevent excessive flexing, the result is a boot which is now standard wear for most hill-walkers and rock-scramblers.

Specialist climbing boots or PAs (lightweight bootees invented by mountain guide Pierre Allain) are not necessary for the beginner; they are ideal for specific use but distinctly limited in other respects. Choose your boots from a specialist supplier who will advise you on the various brands available. Bearing in mind that your feet will expand as you walk, make sure that the boots are over-

size enough to accommodate ragg-wool Norwegian oversocks. Break them in progressively on your local patch before embarking on any extended hill-walk. Dress them thoroughly, though not *too* frequently, with wax proofing (to avoid over-softening), dry them naturally (never on a radiator), and do not leave repairs too late. Treated properly, a good pair of hill-walking boots will pay for themselves many times over.

Clothing

Jeans may be tough, fashionable, and almost universal leisure-wear, but they leave a lot wanting at altitude. Anyone who has suffered a soaking on the hills will know why. For covering the lower limbs, opt for material that will not feel ice-cold when wet and that will deflect at least some of those razor-sharp winds that gust around the tops at times. Twill or wool/fibre slacks are far better. Derby tweed walking trousers or climbing breeches are probably best for all seasons, though inclined to be almost too warm in high summer.

Far left The right footwear is vital for comfortable walking. Boots should be tough but light in weight, and have a patterned sole to give a good grip. Maps and guide-books are essential to any high-country expedition.

Above Jeans are not very practical walking gear. Tweed trousers or climbing breeches (right) are preferable. Boots should be large enough to accommodate oversocks.

Left Clothing for both fair- and wet-weather conditions must be practical and efficient. Waterproof garments must also be windproof; they should not restrict movement.

Protection for the top half of the body is largely a matter of personal choice since the partial demise in popularity of the traditional sail-cloth anorak. Advances in the design of wet-weather gear have shown the quality man-made rainwear to be efficiently windproof, hence almost dual-purpose. For dry-weather warmth, insulation, absorption, and freedom of movement, the onion-skin principle of wearing layers of clothes of natural wool is excellent. These layers can be supplemented during winter with thermal underwear or a padded waist-coat.

All parts of Britain have a high annual rainfall. Among the hills and mountains it is almost a truism that if it is not actually raining, it has just stopped or is threatening. So if you are going to venture into high country, make sure your wet-weather gear really is suitable for the British climate. Paper-thin nylon anoraks may be adequate for strolls in high summer, but serious hill-walkers require something far more substantial.

Waterproofs must obviously live up to their name, but they should be wind-proof too, so that body temperature can be maintained. They must be cut generously to allow freedom of movement and keep condensation to an acceptable minimum. They should also be light-weight, compact, and preferably brightly coloured. This is a common-sense choice not only on the hills, but when road-walking in poor visibility.

These requirements do not come cheaply, but the initial outlay is well worth it. The best-quality rain-suits are tailored from substantial nylon material or waxed cotton. The former are the most popular and although reasonably light and acceptably small when folded, they are stout enough to stand up to long-term wear. They give excellent protection against heavy, prolonged rain, and condensation, which can never be eradicated entirely, is kept to a minimum.

Such over-garments are proofed with several coats of polyurethane or neo-prene and the seams are welded and/or specially treated. Other features are: a heavy-duty zip, itself protected by a flap fastened with Velcro (this not only keeps out the wet but ensures the garment is totally windproof); elasticated and adjustable inner cuffs; spacious pockets designed to prevent water entering; a storm-proof collar; and a generously cut hood with draw-strings.

Over-trousers are no less vital than the coat. However voluminous the top garment, persistent rain will eventually run on to knees and down to socks. Quality over-trousers with long side-zips and an elasticated waist-band which may be slipped on or off without removing your boots will counter this problem. Gaiters, of canvas or nylon, are favoured by some, especially those who climb or rock-scramble, for knee movement remains unrestricted; these are often worn with the longer-length cagoule. This outfit is not totally satisfactory as there is still a gap through which water can penetrate.

Rucksacks

Rainwear, spare woollens, emergency rations, navigation aids: as the small pile grows the next obvious requirement is a rucksack, not only for necessities but also for any personal possessions like camera or binoculars. A small day-pack will be adequate for modest rambles but more adventurous and extended excursions will require a rucksack. Sleeping out is the ideal way of getting to know the countryside in which you are walking, as well as being an enjoyable pastime in itself. It is also easy and surprisingly comfortable, particularly if you take advantage of the wide range of light-weight camping gear now available.

Taken to the limit of independent foot travel over rough country, it is called backpacking. Between day-walking and backpacking there is (for want of a better term) 'week-ending', where the high-country wanderer retains a degree of independence, but relies on available local resources for food and accom-modation such as inns, farms, bed-and-breakfast houses, or youth hostels.

Whatever method you choose, your rucksack will play a very important part in the success and pleasure of your excursion. Like your boots, it will in due course be elevated to the status of a familiar and reliable good companion. Choose a well-made, reputable brand, ensure it really does fit perfectly (there are graded sizes and shapes to suit all heights and builds), and, whatever the temptation, never overload it with even a single item of extraneous equipment.

There are a couple of points to watch when selecting a rucksack. The medium or larger-sized types often have a built-in hip-belt; make sure it is wide enough

and well padded. If you intend climbing or rock-scrambling more than walking, avoid the H-frame pack in favour of the anatomic model with its smoother contours which has a concealed frame. The former, though excellent for the hill-walker with his self-sufficient load, can get caught on rocks and is therefore hazardous on any rock-face. Finally, it is a good idea to protect your possessions in a large plastic bag before putting them into the rucksack; no rucksack is totally waterproof.

Other practical information, from choosing a compass (and learning how to use it), to equipment for first climbing needs, to the complete camping outfit for the high-country explorer, is contained in the bibliography at the end of this book. There is also a list of specialist clubs and organizations which should prove helpful in the early stages of hill-travelling, together with a list of youth hostels in the British Isles.

Fitness

As I have already said, the hills are never far away in the British Isles. Thanks to the topography and the free access to open space, training grounds abound nationwide. There is no better terrain in which to widen knowledge of the outdoors and tune up physically than among hills that are familiar and local.

Week-end hill-walking, coupled with regular exercise, is the key. Getting into shape for extended hill-walking (as opposed to climbing) demands only a reasonable effort to expand the latent capacity of heart, lungs, and muscles. Fifteen or twenty minutes of brisk walking every day, rain or shine, is infinitely preferable to a desperate crash-course on the eve of a holiday.

Embarking on a modest programme of abstinence is also beneficial. If you are overweight (and most of us are in the Western world), cut down a little on sugar and carbohydrates. Nothing drastic is needed, just enough to shed obvious surplus. Instant fitness will not result but over the long term, a slightly more active, slightly less indulgent life will be its own reward, in well-being rediscovered. Where walking may once have been a physical chore, it will now be a pleasant, natural routine, as essential to good health as food and sleep.

Far left The size of rucksack will depend on the type and length of walk you are planning. Choose it with care, and never overload it with unnecessary items.

Left Careful planning and preparation are essential to the success of every excursion. Personal physical fitness should not be overlooked; a short programme of regular exercise will soon show results.

The South Country

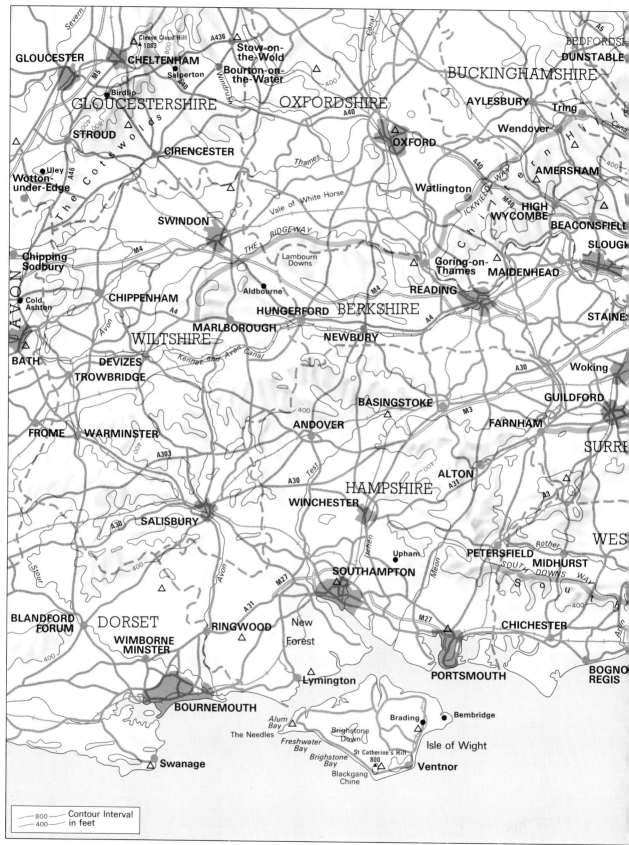

Contour Interval
in feet
— 800 —
— 400 —

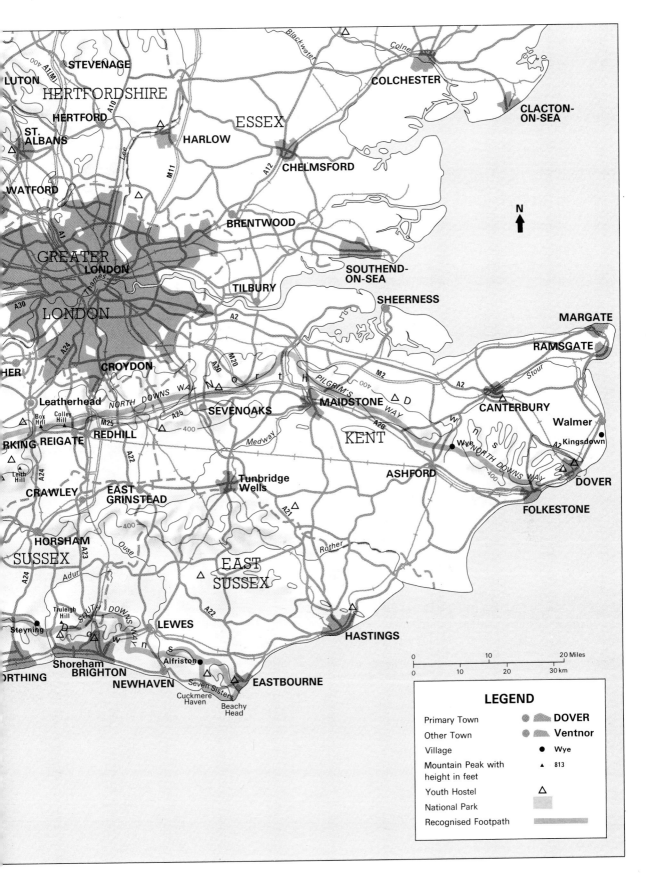

The South-eastern Counties

The North Downs

If I were asked to suggest a stretch of elevated English landscape to encourage the leisure walker, I could hardly improve on what happens to be a local and personal favourite: the footpath which traverses the lofty south-eastern end of the North Downs, better known as The White Cliffs of Dover.

The 8-mile section between the castles of Walmer and Dover is a veritable kaleidoscope of land and seascape, ranging from pastoral downland to the urban bustle of Dover Docks. The seaboard scene alone makes this lofty path memorable, though this is only part of

the attraction. A typical day's walk might start at Walmer Castle, built on the orders of Henry VIII in 1538-40 as one of a string of coastal defences against the threat of a French invasion.

At Walmer, beach-walking gives way abruptly just west of Kingsdown (where there is a pleasant foreshore pub), to an impressive chalk scarp. Sculpted steps provide easy ascent to the cliff-tops above the army firing ranges. Skirting Kingsdown golf course at first, the houses thin away and you are soon striding superb open downland, with the sea far below. On a clear day, the French coastline can be seen in sharp detail.

Right Box Hill in Surrey, rising to 560 feet, is a popular area for outdoor enthusiasts within easy reach of London.

Below St Margaret's Bay, popularly known as The White Cliffs of Dover, is just one fine point along the North Downs Way.

West of St Margaret's Bay (where the path plummets to sea level and rises immediately to the cliff-top again) is the dazzling-white lighthouse where you bear directly seawards and then westwards once more to follow the truly splendid stretch to Dover Heights. Here Dover Castle proclaims itself as the most powerful stronghold in England, save for the Tower of London. The castle grounds extend to some 35 acres within a positively regal setting.

Those wishing to extend the walk from Dover can join the North Downs Way at Shakespeare Cliff and continue along more magnificent cliff paths to the Valiant Sailor pub high above Folkestone. There is a youth hostel at Dover and a camping-ground in a quiet valley setting at Martin Mill, 2 miles inland from St Margaret's Bay.

A few miles north-west of Folkestone lies one of the prettiest backwater valleys in south-east England, the Kentish Stour around Wye. From the centre of this charming village of half-timbered houses a number of paths lead to the great chalk downs rising on the outskirts. Hereabouts the North Downs Way splits to form the Canterbury Loop.

For the finest of the open downs head westwards, away from Wye Agricultural College (founded in the fifteenth century), past the chalk-cut hillside crown, and on up towards the summit near a nature reserve. The historic Pilgrims' Way runs near by and the whole area is rich in exciting archaeological finds, including the giant skeleton of a warrior. Panoramas from the hill ridges are magnificent – over the English Channel in one direction and as far as the borders of Surrey in the other. There is a choice of accommodation at Wye, and a convenient camping-ground just north of Westwell, a village some five miles to the north-west.

One of the best-loved sections of the North Downs Way within easy reach of London covers Box Hill, Colley Hill, and Leith Hill in Surrey and offers one of the most exhilarating viewpoints in the Home Counties. Protected now by the National Trust, the heights of Box Hill, some 560 feet above sea level, are crisscrossed by a confusion of footpaths, but anyone approaching from the A24 Dorking/Leatherhead road can easily spy out the summit routes. There is a minor road called the Zig-Zag, or a direct footpath near Burford Bridge Hotel for the more active.

Those walking the full length of the North Downs Way see the whole beauty of this area which extends through some invigorating undulating country westwards to Colley Hill above Reigate. This majestic scarp vies with Box Hill as a viewpoint ridge and in its way is equally dramatic. Spring, late autumn, or winter are the best times to walk this route which in summer becomes almost too busy with strollers and picnic parties. Outside the high season the area still resembles the natural leisure park it has been since the mid-eighteenth century. For those intending to tackle Britain's sterner hill country, the Box Hill area is an excellent training ground within easy reach of the capital.

There is a youth hostel north-west of Dorking on Ranmore Common. From Leith Hill, at 960 feet the highest point of the North Downs, some five miles south-west of Box Hill, there are far-ranging views from the summit paths. From the eighteenth-century hill-top tower you can see the English Channel on a clear day and that other great hill swathe, the South Downs.

The South Downs

The eastern end of the South Downs could scarcely be more dramatic, dominated as it is by the great chalk bluff of Beachy Head, rising almost directly from sea level to 600 feet, 4 miles west of Eastbourne. Here too is the start of that most celebrated south-country footpath and bridleway, the South Downs Way.

Walkers have the option of going inland towards Wilmington and the north-facing Downs, or choosing the majestic coastal path over the rolling Seven Sisters white cliffs. Inland, beyond Cuckmere Haven and man-made Friston Forest, the two routes converge below Windover Hill and that strange outline, the Long Man.

Both routes are beautiful in their way, both much trodden in summer, but comparative solitude awaits the walker willing to walk on westwards beyond Alfriston to ascend to Firle Beacon. If there is one special place that epitomizes the timeless spendour of the Downs, it is this ridge, the summit 713 feet above sea level, covered with Iron and Bronze Age barrows, creating a magic mix of nature and evidence of early Man.

A walk over the Seven Sisters and a ramble south-west of Firle might well encourage you to tackle the full 80 miles of the South Downs Way. The Way is particularly suitable for newcomers to long-distance walking as the going is easy, there is no risk of getting lost, and there are pockets of civilization in accessible and regular close order along the entire length.

Another high spot worthy of mention is the stretch between Devil's Dyke and Chanctonbury Ring, just to the north-west of Brighton. The Dyke is a splendid downland combe, heavily patronized during summer, with the beech ring of Chanctonbury on the western skyline. Take the up and down route between Steyning and Shoreham and come eventually upon the Iron Age camp capping this 800-foot hill-top. It is from this ring of prehistoric remains that the name derives, and not from the circle of beech-trees, which were only planted in the eighteenth century. The Romans conceivably used the site as a look-out post protecting Stane Street, the link between Chichester, London, and Colchester. Further west Stane Street crosses the South Downs Way and at Bignor there is a Roman villa, one of the largest discovered in Britain containing many superbly restored mosaics.

There are youth hostels at Alfriston, Brighton, and Truleigh Hill; the camping-ground at Sheepcote Valley (Brighton) is strategically located for the South Downs.

Below Chanctonbury Ring dominates the skyline on the South Downs Way north-west of Brighton.

The Isle of Wight

The holiday island of Wight, now often so crowded in summer, has a beautiful and relatively secluded hill line along its southern side, between Bembridge and The Needles. The established Coastal Path traces the entire length (and goes on to encircle the whole island). Near Ventnor is St Catherine's Hill, 800 feet above sea level and the highest point of the island. Below, on the seaward side, stretches that strange tract the Undercliff, a terrace formed by collapsing rocks overlying softer sand and clay strata which have been undermined.

The whole of Wight's chalk ridge was formed by the forward edge of two gigantic billows raised in the earth's crust some 20 million years ago. Originally these were about 4000 feet high, but have been worn away by erosion. Green and very pleasant walking awaits those taking the path above Blackgang Chine, Brightstone Bay, and the Tennyson country between Freshwater Bay and Alum Bay.

Brightstone Down provides a breathtaking 700-foot vantage-point, with a headland camp site that could hardly be better situated for the area, on the seaward side of Brightstone village. Much of this southern coast is now under the care of the National Trust.

Near the eastern end of the island, just south of Brading, is Morton Farm Roman Villa, one of the best-preserved of several scattered across the island. At Brading itself there is the oldest church; it is curiously linked with Wye on the North Downs for in the church grounds yet more giant skeletal remains have been unearthed. There is food for some tantalizing speculation here, perhaps an archaeological lead to a mystery trail of ancient British giants, or some early Scandinavian invaders.

Ordnance Survey maps: 179, 187, 188, 189, 196, 197, 198, 199

Below A splendid coastal path leads over the Seven Sisters cliffs, giving exhilarating seascapes.

Hill-tracks between Thames and Severn

The Chiltern Hills

Not far west of central London lies Goring-on-Thames, as significant a spot on the map today for those wishing to escape from the metropolis as it was for early foot-travellers, for it was once a major river-crossing for pilgrims as well as a natural route through the hills. North-west of the Goring Gap rise the Chiltern Hills, those summit ridges following one after another to Ivinghoe Beacon which form part of the Ridgeway Path. The Ridgeway, which extends through five counties of southern England, is ideal walking terrain, well defined and never exceeding 1000 feet.

Below the Chiltern escarpment stretch the Icknield Ways, ancient green lanes dating back to prehistoric times that can be followed beyond the Chilterns through Dunstable and to far-off East Anglia. To the west, between the Wessex North Downs and the Vale of the White Horse, the Ridgeway is not only beautiful, sometimes spectacularly so, it is also the oldest footway in Britain.

Walking the Icknield Way in the vicinity of Shirburn Hill, north-east of Watlington, is to see the glory of Chiltern beech-woods at their best, especially in autumn. Some of these giants that grace the slopes are over 150 years old. The beeches are just one of the natural attractions of the area, for while the Chilterns are only modest compared to most hills (the highest summit is Coombe Hill above Wendover, just over 840 feet), the landscape is infinitely variable. Rolling dome-tops, patchwork arable farms, and magnificent tall trees combine to give fine hill-walking for both the novice and the more experienced enthusiast.

Christmas Common, a mile or so from Shirburn Hill, is a favoured picnic area of high terrain from which radiate numerous footpaths, all offering splendid views. Watlington is a very old and pleasing Oxfordshire town, with good accommodation and a friendly pub, The Carriers, well known to walkers.

If you follow the Ridgeway north-east you come eventually upon Ivinghoe Beacon, the site of an Iron Age fort and signal-fire pinnacle. Now half encircled by the encroachment of urban Tring, it is none the less a fitting landscape marker to the northern end of the Ridgeway Path, especially when approached from those rolling Chiltern Hills to the south-west. Here, the ancient Icknield Ways join and continue (now a single metalled road) to Dunstable and beyond.

The footpath east of Tring, which ascends from the Grand Union Canal and railway station, is an impressive ascent. It is also gratifyingly scenic along the ridge of Pitstone Hill and Ivinghoe Hills to the Beacon, where vistas extend to every point of the compass. The National Trust protect much of this area, though regrettably they are fighting a losing battle in some respects for the Beacon is scarred by many seemingly aimless paths. Avoid this hill if you can on high days and holidays when the Chilterns around Ivinghoe are heavily, if understandably, pressed. There are youth hostels at Goring and Ivinghoe.

Right The Ridgeway, south of Britwell Salome near Watlington, where the Path passes through the beautiful Chiltern beech-woods.

Below White Horse Hill, near Wantage, is a celebrated landmark along the Ridgeway Path.

The Cotswolds

The Old English word for sheep-pen is cote, while wold simply means weald. Therefore the name 'Cotswold' could hardly be more apt for the friendly green hills which span that area east of the Severn between Bath and Broadway. Once the great sheep-rearing district of England, today little remains of the vast pastoral industry of 500 years ago. Sheep do still graze of course, but the real miracle is that the lush wooded uplands have escaped the worst ravages of progress. What those influential sheep barons have left to posterity is a host of golden-stone towns and hamlets within the landscape that actually retains a surprising element of its natural, medieval virtues. It is a combination that has come to epitomize the unchanging English countryside for other nations.

The hills themselves cannot compare with those soaring giants west of the Severn in Wales – the highest of them are only around 1000 feet high. The sudden upthrust from the valley floors of some of the escarpments is nevertheless spectacular enough. There are pleasing visual surprises around almost every bend along the numerous hill-top roads.

The area is somewhat loosely defined geographically, since the hills stretch from Worcestershire to Somerset and from Herefordshire to Oxfordshire, but the heart of the Cotswolds lies in Gloucestershire and it is this county which boasts most of the scenic gems. For a strategic, indeed delightful base I would choose Wotton-Under-Edge, not far from the Wildfowl Trust at Slimbridge. North of Chipping Sodbury, in the land triangle formed by the arms of the M4 and M5, there is a strategic caravan park. Located just west of Wotton and signposted between the B4058 and B4060, it offers excellent facilities for caravanners and campers, and the setting, under the Westridge spur of the Cotswolds with views across to Wales, is positively therapeutic. There is fine walking near by, through some 2000 acres of hill woodland, with the old-world village of Wotton just along the road. For one of the most impressive of south Cotswold ridges, take the minor road north-east towards Stroud.

At Coaley Peak View Point there is a majestic downland sweep affording eagle-eye views of the surrounding countryside. Uley village, not far from here, is a worthwhile target for walkers, with an Iron Age fort just above and Uley Tumulus (popularly known as

Above Upper Slaughter, a village on the Cotswold plateau, where streams wind through green and peaceful valleys.

Hetty Pegler's Tump), near by. It is a popular spot for flying enthusiasts.

From Stroud – itself surrounded by beautiful hill country and once the capital of Britain's broad-cloth industry – the B4070 passes through Birdlip where there is a pleasing stretch of the Cotswold Way long-distance footpath. The road goes on to Cheltenham, one of the grandest spa towns in all Europe.

Three miles north of the town is Cleeve Cloud Hill and Common, at 1083 feet the highest point of the Cotswolds, dominating the skyline above the villages of Woodmancote and Bishops Cleeve. To the south of Cheltenham is one of the most dramatic of all Cotswold outcrops, the Devil's Chimney, a strangely shaped, impressive rock pinnacle. To reach it, take the B4070 for 2 miles, then fork towards Salterley Grange and walk the Cotswold

Way path for about a quarter of a mile.

From Cheltenham, it is another delight to cross the Cotswold range eastwards by some superb and largely unused minor roads, the lure perhaps being Bourton-on-the-Water or Broadway. Both are gold-stone clusters (the first with lawn-edged streets bordering the sparkling Windrush, the second one of England's jealously preserved heritage villages), but both are oppressed with visitors in summer.

A less crowded, more out-of-the-way excursion is to take the footpath between Salperton and Cold Aston, south of the A436. Here you will find that sheep country as it has been for centuries, a landscape of pastures, dry-stone walls,

Above A panoramic view over the Cotswold countryside from the Iron Age fort above Uley village.

arable sweeps, and wooded knolls, dissected by lanes of ancient origin and dotted hamlets tucked high in the hills.

Salperton itself was on an old salt route (hence its name) which probably ran from Droitwich to the Thames and from there by waterway to London. One source of the Thames is only a few miles south-west of Cirencester, still the hub of the southern Cotswolds as it was in ancient times; for here is the meeting point of Fosse Way, Ermine Way, and Akeman Street.

South-east from the Cotswold Hills, Ermine Way arrows through Cirencester, the second largest city of Roman Britain, and bypasses Swindon to enter the Vale of the White Horse. From here, a minor road, the B4507, winds east to the hamlet of Letcombe Bassett, the starting-point of a very exciting hill walk and a fitting finale to this selection of

southern English uplands.

So far, many of the high spots mentioned have been localized, but for the more ambitious walker, this stretch of the Cotswolds offers some thirty miles of the Ridgeway long-distance footpath. It is a week-end walk as memorable as any in Britain (or anywhere else for that matter), not only for its scenic beauty, but also because in places it is an uncanny encounter across time.

Letcombe Bassett, a cluster of racing stables and picture-book thatched cottages, lies in a warm valley beneath a regal sweep of Lambourn Downs. Minor lanes and tracks provide a due-south ascent to the Ridgeway, which is joined between Segsbury Camp and the Devil's Punchbowl. The first is an Iron Age earthworks, the second a natural scallop and prehistoric river-course. It is the approach and ascent of White Horse

Hill, however, that is the first pearl in this string of successive visual delights.

Here the lofty path reaches 850 feet, revealing just below that most elegant and striking of all Britain's chalk-cut figures, the famous White Horse. Its origins are uncertain; it may have been cut in the Iron Age, or possibly around 800 AD. Almost adjacent is the unmistakable Dragon Hill, flat-topped and chalk-scarred, and the Manger, another massive earth scallop, while beyond are vistas which seem to extend halfway across England. Uffington Castle earthworks, ancient but unspectacular, lie just to the north of the Ridgeway at this point.

A mile or so further, in a splendidly isolated location alongside the path, is Wayland's Smith Cave, invariably known as Wayland's Smithy. This chambered long barrow, built around 3000 BC, really does bring home to the foot-traveller the age of this track-way. Perhaps it is the setting, among a handsome stand of trees in a wide, arable prairie, perhaps the silence of the lonely heights, or the magnificent preserved state of the ancient tomb which gives rise to this sensation. But its effect, particularly in the early morning, is undeniable. Attached to the place is the legend, probably of Anglo-Saxon origin, of the ghostly smith who was never seen but who would shoe any horse left overnight, along with the appropriate fee.

Some four miles further along the Path, after entering Wiltshire and negotiating Charlbury and Fox hills, you cross the M4 motorway. Almost at once, however, you are by the Shepherd's Rest Inn and alongside the Roman Ermine Way. The downland route between Swindon and Marlborough passes by Liddington Castle, just one of a whole succession of Iron Age earthworks along or alongside the Ridgeway Path.

From the ridge of Round Hill Down you can see the far-off Cotswolds as you ascend again to over 800 feet. East of the Path is the Giant's Grave, one of many barrows between Upham and Aldbourne. The Path descends once more, this time to the straggling hamlet of Ogbourne St George, along many surfaced roads and an oppressive stretch of densely hedged lane. From there it ascends to reach Smeathe's Ridge, a fine chalk scarp nearly 700 feet high, and yet another earthworks, the clearly defined Iron Age Barbury Castle, stronghold of the Anglo-Saxon chieftain Bera.

So to the long, exhilarating descent of

Hackpen Hill, the track high, wide, and most handsome. The Path is dotted increasingly with wayside sarsen stones, culminating at the foot of Overton Hill with the end of the Ridgeway. A host of prehistoric wonders are to be found here: West Kennett long barrow, one of the largest and finest in Britain, a huge chalk-mound burial chamber some 350 feet long; four Neolithic stone circles, of which dramatic Avebury is one; the mysterious mound of Silbury Hill, once linked to Avebury by a mile-long avenue of megaliths. The whole is bisected by the Roman road to Bath, adding a further historical dimension to this rich area.

Ordnance Survey maps: 150, 162, 163, 164, 165, 166, 172, 173, 174, 175

Above Broadway Hill (1024 feet), to the south of Broadway and crowned by a tower that is a landmark for many miles around, gives superb views over the surrounding countryside.

Left The Cotswold landscape is characterized by lush wooded uplands, once the great sheep-rearing district of England.

Wales

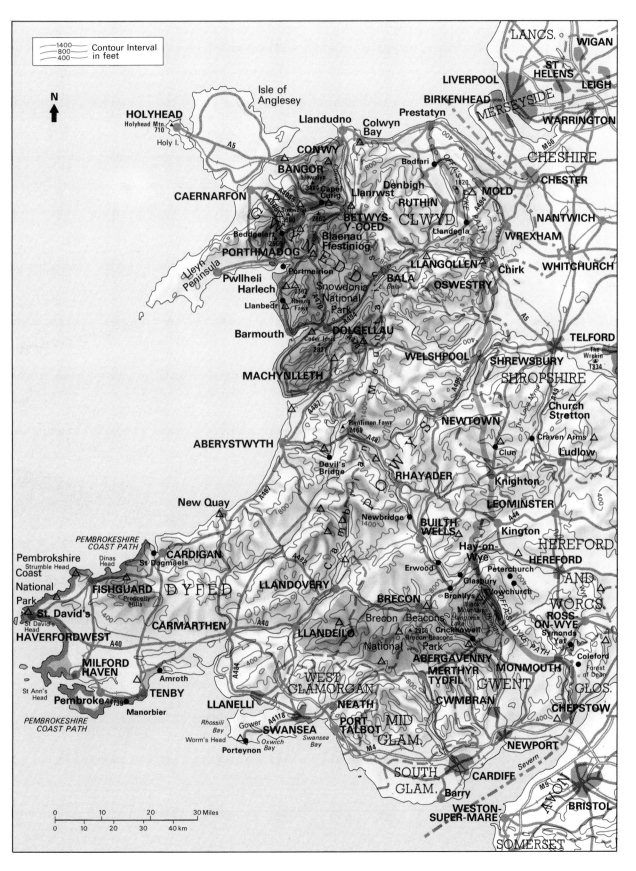

Contour Interval in feet
1400
800
400

N

LANCS.

WIGAN

ST HELENS

LEIGH

LIVERPOOL

BIRKENHEAD

Prestatyn

MERSEYSIDE

WARRINGTON

CHESHIRE

Isle of Anglesey

HOLYHEAD
Holyhead Mtn
710
Holy I.

A5

Llandudno

Colwyn Bay

CONWY

BANGOR

Llewlyn
3484

Capel Curig

Llanrwst

Denbigh

Bodfari

CHESTER

NANTWICH

MOLD
1820

RUTHIN

CLWYD

Llandegla

WREXHAM

WHITCHURCH

CAERNARFON

Snowdon
3560

BETWYS-Y-COED

Beddgelert
2566

Blaenau Ffestiniog

LLANGOLLEN

Chirk

OSWESTRY

PORTHMADOG

Portmeirion

Lleyn Peninsula

Pwllheli
Harlech

2382

Llanbedr

Rhinog Fawr
2362

Snowdonia National Park

BALA
L. Bala

DOLGELLAU

Barmouth

Cader Idris
2921

A5

TELFORD

The Wrekin
T334

WELSHPOOL

SHREWSBURY

SHROPSHIRE

MACHYNLLETH

The Long Mynd

ABERYSTWYTH

Plynlimon Fawr
2468

A44

Devil's Bridge

NEWTOWN

Church Stretton

Craven Arms

Ludlow

Clun

RHAYADER

Knighton

LEOMINSTER

New Quay

Newbridge
1400

BUILTH WELLS

Kington

HEREFORD

HEREFORD

CARDIGAN

St Dogmaels

PEMBROKESHIRE COAST PATH

Dinas Head

Hay-on-Wye

Erwood

Peterchurch

AND

Strumble Head

Pembrokeshire Coast National Park

FISHGUARD

DYFED

Prescelly Hills

LLANDOVERY

Glasbury

Bronllys

Vowchurch

WORCS.

ROSS-ON-WYE

Symonds Yat

St David's
St David's Head

HAVERFORDWEST

A40

CARMARTHEN

A40

LLANDEILO

BRECON

Black Mountains

Llangorse Lake

Brecon Beacons
2906

Crickhowell

Coleford

Brecon Beacons National Park

ABERGAVENNY

MONMOUTH

Forest of Dean

GLOS.

St Ann's Head

MILFORD HAVEN

Amroth

TENBY

LLANELLI

WEST GLAMORGAN

NEATH

MERTHYR TYDFIL

CWMBRAN

GWENT

CHEPSTOW

Pembroke
A4139

Manorbier

Rhossili Bay

Gower

Worm's Head

Oxwich Bay

SWANSEA

Swansea Bay

PORT TALBOT

MID GLAM.

M4

NEWPORT

PEMBROKESHIRE COAST PATH

Porteynon

SOUTH GLAM.

CARDIFF

Severn

Barry

WESTON-SUPER-MARE

M5

BRISTOL

SOMERSET

0   10   20   30 Miles

0   10   20   30   40 km

41

The Wye Valley and Mid-Wales

The Wye Valley

By travelling west and crossing the Severn estuary into Wales you come upon a very different landscape from the soft, rounded contours of southern England. Here the terrain is much more dramatic, ranging scenically from the impressive to the majestic, seldom if ever dull or – far worse – over-developed by man.

In the Principality, the first of the true mountains come under review. Not immediately, however, for, like all fine things, the prospect is best savoured through gradual elevation to those soaring heights. By way of a preliminary I can think of no more exhilarating approach route to mid-Wales than through the Wye Valley, as it is blessed with three ingredients that make up a near-perfect natural mix: a fast-flowing river punctuated by reaches of rushing white water; lush green hills that come very close to mountains in places; and the great swathe of the Forest of Dean which has changed little in centuries.

There are certain places where the number of people does become excessive at times – Symonds Yat is one of them – but this should not deter the first-time visitor from enjoying the natural beauties of the area. From Symonds Yat Rock, for instance, there are panoramas of no less than seven counties on a clear day, together with a majestic snake-like sweep of the river seen almost immediately below. The boundaries of the Wye Valley Beauty Area (which was designated in 1971) encompass only some 125 square miles of Gloucestershire, Gwent, Herefordshire, and Worcestershire, but few comparable areas of the British Isles offer such a wide diversity of landscape.

The gateway is Chepstow, that ancient walled town that dominates the southern end of the Wye and boasts one of the mightiest Norman strongholds in the land. Just a few miles north-east is the Royal Forest of Dean, one of the very few places in these islands where woodland cover has existed continuously in a relatively unaltered state for many thousands of years.

There is spacious camping in the heart of the Forest at Christchurch, near Coleford, administered by the Forestry Commission. This is an ideal base from which to make walking forays of the area. In early spring or late autumn the Forest is at its best and the many superb trails and waymarked walks are relatively deserted, so make a virtue of necessity and go early or late in the year if you can. The route-marked walks are graded to suit every age and capability.

The river-valley path to Symonds Yat Rock is predictably the most frequented, but there is a whole trail of historical evidence within the forest confines: King Arthur's Caves in Lord's Wood, where evidence of prehistoric man has been found; the iron-ore shafts of Clearwell Caves, dug during the Roman occupation; disused coal-mine workings of the last century.

Coleford itself dates back to the reign of Charles II, and the tiny Severn port of Lydney, a short distance away, was once the site of a Roman temple. Perhaps most fascinating of all is the southern section of Offa's Dyke, which begins just outside Chepstow on the banks of the Severn and continues – albeit intermittently – all the way to the North Wales coast near Prestatyn.

There is a rampart section of this great defensive earthworks at Symonds Yat, and another above Tintern Abbey. Built on the orders of Offa, King of Mercia, in the eighth century, the Dyke was a frontier-marker dividing Mercia from the various Welsh kingdoms. Some 81 miles of the earthworks can still be traced, and there is one unbroken stretch of 60 miles, from Kington to Chirk. Offa's Dyke Path, the long-distance route which runs the length of the English-Welsh border, follows the Dyke closely along this stretch.

From bustling Ross-on-Wye it is possible to take a route almost free of traffic through a charming – and comparatively unknown – area of Herefordshire. Between Vowchurch and Peterchurch, in the aptly named Golden Valley, there is a camping-park which gives views of the Black Mountains on one side and the Wye Valley on the other. Those Black Mountains, with the Brecon Beacons dominating the centre, extend in a grand succession of ridges, almost to the Swansea valleys.

This is, as it were, the back-door entrance to Mid-Wales, and a most exciting one. For by tracing a road route carefully with the aid of appropriate Ordnance Survey maps – and with frequent pedestrian excursions – you can remain amid rural Wales much as Cobbett must have known it.

An interesting start is to follow the back lanes from the vicinity of Golden Valley to the picturesque town of Hay-on-Wye. Once a border fortress settlement, it is Hay's strategic location, nestling under the northern scarp of the Black Mountains, that is of interest to the hill-walker. Take the lane and then the Offa's Dyke Path south of the town to Hay Bluff, for one of the most stimulating eyrie viewpoints anywhere along the English-Welsh border. Indeed, if you follow the high route further, southeast above the river Honddu, you will cross Hatterrall Ridge, one of the finest mountain-top sections of the entire Dyke Path.

Between Hay and Llanfihangel-Crucorney, almost midway along this easternmost sky-scraper ridge of the Black Mountains, which in places reaches 2000 feet and more, are the ruins of the twelfth-century Llanthony Priory in its classically beautiful setting in a green and wooded valley with the skyline ridge towering dramatically above. There is a convenient camping-ground near by and a youth hostel just north of Llanthony.

Left Symonds Yat is a deservedly popular tourist attraction within the Wye Valley Beauty Area. There are wide panoramic views from the top of the limestone cliffs.

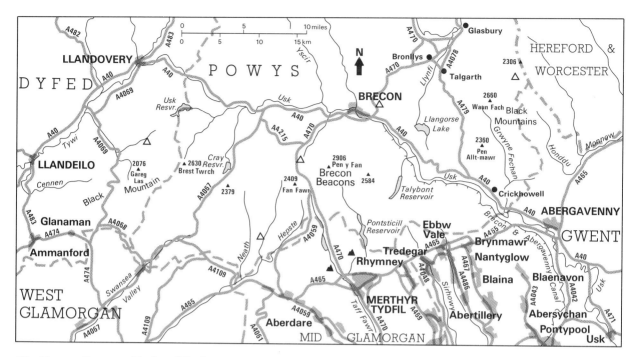

The Brecon Beacons National Park

Llangorse Lake, set in the green Usk Valley, is a bird-watchers' paradise which, more prosaically, has a number of camping-grounds, making it a favoured base for visitors to the Brecon Beacons National Park. South-west of Brecon is the Libanus Mountain Centre which provides an excellent source of local information, particularly for those wishing to take advantage of this superb walking area and explore the surrounding country on foot. Just a short stroll away from here is a stretch of the Roman road, Sarn Helen, which once linked South and North Wales.

The A470 south from Libanus will bring you to Storey Arms, some nine miles from Breacon, and the start of the ascent to the summit of Pen y Fan, at 2906 feet the giant of the National Park. This is a superb hill-walk over sheep-cropped turf for much of the distance. There is no scrambling involved, but one or two pitches are fairly steep, although this should not be a deterrent to anyone who is reasonably fit. The route is well marked but this is nevertheless not a climb to be attempted in doubtful weather. On a clear day, from the summit you can see as far as the Bristol Channel and even beyond to the hills of Devon. The total distance from road to summit is about three miles.

These great ridge-backs that form the Black Mountains and Brecon Beacons are Devonian, named after Devon where

rocks of this age (around 300 million years) are well exposed, hard enough to withstand a great deal of erosion. If they were of softer material, such as limestone, the lofty Beacons of today might just be another group of softly contoured hills. As it is, they are among the most spectacular of Britain's mountain ranges, with a great wealth of natural and manmade attractions.

The Black Mountains

West of the Brecon Beacons, across Fforest Fawr, is the Black Mountain (singular) and a stretch of genuine wilderness across the tops, where some twenty-five square miles of wind-swept moorland are untouched by roads. Just two of the many gems worth seeing are the Llyn-y-Fan Fach, a startlingly beautiful glacial lake surrounded by 500-foot cliffs; and Carreg Cennen, a thirteenth-century fortress ruin standing on a great limestone crag at the extreme western end of the Black Mountain.

North of Brecon a very pleasant route follows the river Honddu alongside the B4520 for much of the way to Builth Wells, and on to Rhayader, one of the great pony-trekking centres of Mid-Wales. This is an ideal area for those who prefer saddles to walking-boots. From here it is not far to some of the least-frequented high country in Britain. Westwards towards the Powis-Salop border there are invigorating vistas

around Radnor Forest and along the north-south line of Offa's Dyke Path between Kington and Knighton. Knighton, 'The Town on the Dyke', is the natural midway point of the long-distance path.

It was here that the footpath route was officially opened by Sir John Hunt in 1971. Appropriately enough, the town is also the headquarters of the Offa's Dyke Association. Up the hill from the Clock Square is an information centre and a youth hostel housed in the Old Primary School. The Path immediately north of Knighton, above the walls of the castle ruins, is particularly interesting, not only for the hill scenery, but also because it is the start of the longest almost unbroken stretch of Dyke, extending to the foot of Long Mountain, near Welshpool.

Opposite Walkers on the summit of Pen y Fan, the highest point in the Brecons.

Below From Black Mountain cliffs drop 500 feet into the beautiful Llyn-y-Fan Fach.

The Cambrian Mountains

North-westwards, between Rhayader and the coast at Aberystwyth, lie the Cambrian Mountains. They are not quite as spectacular as the peaks of neighbouring Snowdonia, but still impressive, especially the Plynlimon group. The highest peak is Plynlimon Fawr, rising to 2468 feet above the Nant-y-Moch reservoir. There is a fine and fairly easy ascent route which starts alongside the A44, 5 miles north-east of Devil's Bridge, at Eisteddfa-Gurig Farm. A clearly marked miners' track leads past old lead-mine workings to the summit, giving splendid views across Wales and beyond into Shropshire. It should perhaps be added that this climb should only be attempted in fair weather. If you have any doubts, then there is some particularly pleasant walking of the gentler kind south-west of Rhayader, along the winding Elan Valley which can be followed for 9 miles.

The reservoirs of Garreg-ddu, Craig Goch, and Pen-y-Garreg, which lie in the valley, are more attractive than might be expected, since landscaping has been meticulous and sympathetic. Devil's Bridge has deservedly long been a very popular beauty spot, but not far from the celebrated trio of bridges which span the Mynach Falls you can find much wild, secluded beauty simply by following the Rheidol river and taking the footpath above Rheidol Gorge.

Right The wild gorge where the rivers Mynach and Rheidol join at Devil's Bridge, a famous beauty spot.

The Wye Valley Walk

As a fitting finale to this hill country – which is after all some of the wildest in Wales – I would recommend the Wye Valley Walk. This is a very appropriate choice for those who hanker to be among mountains, yet prefer to take a relatively easy-going valley route. Reaches of the more remote Upper Wye are traced by this 36-mile path, which begins at Hay-on-Wye and then veers north-west through Glasbury, Erwood, Builth Wells, Newbridge, finishing at Rhayader. The surroundings are varied and magnificent all the way, with some fine vistas of the Black Mountain foothills and the wooded valley. Between Hay and Erwood is Maesyronen Chapel, claimed to be the oldest place of Christian worship in Wales, while between Erwood and Builth there is the inn where Henry Mayhew had the brilliant idea of founding *Punch*.

Builth Wells has been a spa resort since Roman times and just north of the town are the Penddol Rocks and Rapids. There is an easy climb to 1000 feet on the way to Newbridge, with sweeping summit views, then the path follows lanes and more heady heights before the final descent to the market town of Rhayader.

There are pleasant camping-grounds scattered throughout Mid-Wales, notably at Bronllys, Rhayader, Talgarth, and Crickhowell, with many rural pitches between towns, invariably amid beautiful surroundings. The area is also well served by youth hostels, particularly amid the Cambrian Mountains and the Brecon Beacons.

Ordnance Survey maps: 135, 136, 146, 147, 148, 160, 161, 162, 171

Below A wide sweep of countryside near Hay-on-Wye, the start of the Hay Valley Walk.

South and West Wales

The Gower Peninsula

The first time I visited the Gower Peninsula it was more or less by accident, making a detour on the way to the Pembrokeshire coast. Yet it is a detour that I would certainly recommend, if only to see the splendour of Rhossili Down and Worm's Head. Leave the west-bound M4 motorway at Exit 47, then join the A484 and make your way into almost instant serenity. It is its comparative isolation, away from the main stream of traffic, that keeps the Gower relatively free of cars and crowds, though it is a popular spot with holiday-makers from Swansea.

There is not a single town of any size on the whole Peninsula. It is a landscape of tiny hamlets, linked by winding narrow lanes and punctuated by some of the most exciting headlands in Britain. Bounded on the eastern side by Swansea Bay, westwards by Rhossili Bay, and north by the Burry Inlet, it is almost more of an island than a peninsula, despite its proximity to the industrial and commercial centres of Port Talbot and Swansea.

For a delightful base, take the A4118 west from Swansea for some eight miles, to the hamlet of Penmaen. There is a farm camping-ground here in a beautiful cliff-top setting, overlooking one of the prettiest natural inlets in Wales. Three

Cliffs Bay is a splash of golden sand, spectacular rock outcrops, and magnificent cliffs; the Bay is free of cars as there is no approach road.

While Oxwich Bay is one of the Peninsula's nature reserves with many protected dunes and woodlands, Port Eynon is arguably the most picturesque of Gower villages. Reached by steep and narrow approach lanes off the A4118, there is some holiday development and a choice of touring-sites. More importantly, the Port Eynon area is a walker's delight. There are numerous footpaths along the cliff-tops and foreshore and not far away at the western end of the Peninsula is one of the most majestic of all headlands in the British Isles, Rhossili and Worm's Head. You can walk from Llangennith across Rhossili Down – the highest point on the Peninsula – earning splendid views from the summit beacon, south-west to Lundy Island and north to Pembrokeshire.

Right The majestic Worm's Head, seen here from the Rhossili cliffs, is the highest point on the Peninsula.

Below A footpath winding through some spectacular cliff scenery to Mewslade Bay.

Pembrokeshire

Once you have left Swansea and the heavy industry of West Glamorgan behind, you enter an area of rural Wales that continues virtually unbroken to the Atlantic seaboard. It is not surprising that this area is a much-loved favourite, for the Pembrokeshire Coast National Park, with its wide vistas, rugged coasts, and fine sand beaches, captivates many people and makes it their particular first choice of hill-country terrain.

The high ground here is mainly coastal, though the Presely Hills are a fascinating exception. The Pembrokeshire coast stretches for some 350 miles, and offers various scenic high spots. The cliffs that bound the coast are not particularly high (the highest are only some 550 feet above sea level), but they seem very lofty and are nearly always dramatic in formation. Anyone who has walked the length, or even part, of the Pembrokeshire Coast Path (St Dogmaels to Amroth, a distance of 168 miles) will surely agree. All coastal heights which I shall mention fall within the National Park which, with an area of 225 square miles, is the smallest in Britain.

The spectacular cliff formations are of particular geological interest, being made up of a mixture of hard bed-rock blended with volcanic lava, coal shales, sandstone, and a fair percentage of carboniferous limestone.

The area also has an interesting historical background as it was here that the Norman conquest of Wales over nine hundred years ago met with least resistance. The Norman influence is marked by the chain of castles in the southern part of the area; Manorbier is the most well known. Pembroke was colonized with Flemish farm-workers in 1090, and to this day the area has retained a separate identity from the rest of Wales. The English atmosphere is particularly marked in Tenby, which is popularly known as Little England Beyond Wales and has been a favoured resort and watering place since Victorian times. Tenby is a good place to begin any upland survey of the National Park, for close by are some very attractive high spots. There is a wide variety of accommodation available, including many touring and holiday parks.

Left Near Elegug Stacks, west of St Govan's Head, one of the many fine high spots along this section of the Pembrokeshire Coast Path.

Tenby Tourist Office, open every day during summer, has a good selection of literature on local walks, though the visitor eager to see some of the best scenery in the vicinity could hardly better the Pembrokeshire Coast Path. The 10-mile stretch between Tenby and Manorbier is particularly interesting and is a good way of gently loosening the muscles before tackling the more rugged parts of the coast. The route takes in Giltar Point and Lydstep Haven below a distinctive headland and although some road-walking is required to skirt an army camp at Old Castle Head, the Path is soon rejoined above Manorbier Castle.

Alongside the Path, at Priest's Nose Point, there is The King's Quoit, a Neolithic burial chamber dating from around 3000 BC. Just inland from the bay lies Manorbier Castle, one of the best-preserved examples of Norman architecture in Wales; it was the birthplace (c.1146) of Giraldus Cambrensis, the celebrated Welsh historian and scribe who left a priceless record of what life in Wales was like during the twelfth century.

A little further west, between Stackpole Quay and The Green Bridge, is a particularly fine stretch of unspoiled and often sheer limestone cliff. The high spots come in quick succession: Stackpole Head, St Govan's Head, the tiny St Govan's Chapel wedged deep among the cliffs. Then follows some splendid flat open-cliff walking to the majestic Stack Rocks and The Green Bridge. Here, unfortunately, the Path turns inland to avoid army firing ranges.

For the next elevated coastal gem, take the A4139 through Pembroke, where the castle – a towering monument to Norman domination – still dwarfs all other buildings in this walled harbour town. A superb stone pile in a magnificent state of preservation, it is a landmark of history well worth stopping to see. From here the main tourist route follows the A477 to Haverfordwest and on to St David's, but misses a superb stretch of coast southwards, around St Ann's Head and Wooltack Point. Detour if you can via the B4327, for offshore are Skomer and Skokholm, reminders of the Viking presence in this area between the eighth and tenth centuries.

This is a wild and exciting coast walk, particularly from Marloes Sands (where there is a youth hostel) round Wooltack Point. The rugged offshore islands are now nature reserves and the haunt of countless sea-birds. From the Path you

can see Jack Sound, where grey seals bask. Marloes Sands is renowned for its lava bread, alias edible seaweed.

So to St David's, birthplace of the patron saint of Wales, and the smallest cathedral city in the British Isles. The cathedral is memorable not only for its beauty, but also for its setting in a deep hollow between the city and the sea so that its tower would not be visible to the marauding Viking raiders.

The coast is equally memorable. St David's Head is just one example of the many majestic headlands here, over-looking Ramsay Island with its seal colony and fringing a vast sweep of the Atlantic ocean. Right to the outskirts of Fishguard the seaboard is fascinating and full of scenic surprises, as those who care to explore by car along the little-used side road will quickly discover. Better still, leave the car and follow any

of the sections of the Coast Path between the two towns. There are cliff-walks here to stimulate the most jaded palate, though most are fairly energetic in part. A pleasant base will be found at the hamlet of Croesgoch, about 1½ miles inland, where there is a touring-site.

From St David's Head the views are as dramatic as any on the whole Path, though the going is easy along this stretch as far as Porth-gain. From here to Strumble Head, however, the Path gets progressively more challenging. There are two youth hostels along this 14-mile section – at Trevine and Pwllderi – and from the latter the walking is tough but magnificent. It is a remote and exhilarating stretch, with majestic cliffs and crashing surf below, probably your only company wild sea-birds wheeling overhead. Around Strumble Head the going becomes briefly even

rougher; this is no place for novices or those out of condition. The lighthouse on the wind-swept point dates from 1908.

The Path continues over rough terrain past Carregwastad Point, though the going gradually becomes easier and the walker is rewarded with fine views over Fishguard Bay and the attractive old town. All along this coastline the cliff path is punctuated with evidence of prehistoric relics of the days when trade and travel was primarily by sea. Burial chambers, Iron Age forts, and religious clues reflect the names of those early Celtic migrants from Ireland who carried Christianity to Wales between the fifth and eighth centuries.

Even today the walker can feel an almost tangible awe of the landscape which remains totally untamed in places. These shores must have been as in-hospitable as any in the world for those

early travellers. Walking under lowering cloud and with the wind piping, one can only marvel at their toughness and tenacity. A fascinating relic of this bygone age is to be found in Mynydd Preseli, the Presely Hills, an impressive hinterland tract south-east of Fishguard.

In terms of elevation the Hills are not exceptional (Presely Top is 1760 feet high), but you can see Ireland on a clear day and, as a piece of almost untouched holy land, it is unique. Dotted with Stone Age, Bronze Age, and Iron Age remains, this wild and wind-swept terrain was once obviously of great importance. Today it is still a remote and little-visited area, where wild ponies roam and the only evidence of modern man are the scattered hill-farms. A contrast to bustling Fishguard, scarcely 10 miles away.

The ancient importance of the area is underlined by the fact that the inner 'blue stones' of Stonehenge originated from the Presely Hills; there is proof of a track-way linking St David's and Salisbury Plain.

Finally, back to the coast and a natural cliff-girt gem close to Fishguard. Climb the steep hill north-eastwards out of the old town until you come to Dinas Head where there is a camping-ground well placed for exploring Dinas Island, once an island but now joined to the mainland. The path which encircles the island covers about four miles of easy, pleasant going, leading over magnificent cliffs; the stack of Needle Rock is just one of several intriguing rock formations. On a sunny day this is a delightful stroll which somehow encapsulates all the regal grandeur of the wilder Welsh coast.

Ordnance Survey maps: 145, 157, 158, 159

Above The coastline around Strumble Head offers a rough but exhilarating stretch of Path.

Above left Limestone rocks near St Govan's Chapel on the southern tip of Pembrokeshire.

North Wales

The Snowdonia National Park

Parc Cenedlaethol Eryri means in English 'The Land of Eagles', and surely no name could be more apt for this northern region of Wales. There are no less than eight mountain ranges within the Snowdonia National Park, with Y Wyddfa (Snowdon) just one of fourteen massive peaks exceeding 3000 feet. Here in a rocky world of soaring passes and steep valleys scoured by Ice Age glaciers, climbers and hill-walkers find challenges as exciting as any in western Europe.

This 845-square-mile 'park' is only one designated area of North Wales high country, which also boasts the Clwydian range to the east of Denbigh; parts of the off-shore island of Anglesey; and the relatively little-visited 'Land's End of the Principality', the Lleyn Peninsula. It is, however, the National Park and that central massif that captivates all those who love the high and wilder parts of these islands.

For any lowland southerner, the first sight of central Snowdonia is unforgettable. The visual impact of this mountain region is a scenic revelation best enjoyed initially when the weather is kindly and the light bright. It is difficult to comprehend that this breath-taking landscape – legacy of volcanic explosions when the world was young – is part of the same land-mass that includes those soft-contoured southern wealds and vast sweeps of East Anglia.

Repeated visits may lessen surprise but it never disappears entirely, and each trip reveals some new and always majestic aspect for the hill-walker ready to roam the more remote heights or steep and half-hidden valleys. All approach routes from the east are full of scenic drama, too, some quite exceptionally beautiful. South through the Dovey Valley and around Cader Idris to Dolgellau is one classic example; the central route via Lake Bala to Blaenau Ffestiniog another.

A third route, outstanding for the diversity of its scenery, is via the A5 through Betws-y-Coed and on under the very shadow of Mount Snowdon, and from there down the great pass to Llanberis. It is often difficult for the first-time visitor to know where best to make a base among so many riches of high-country grandeur. Perhaps Beddgelert takes pride of place, certainly with the camping fraternity, for here amid a wealth of forest and mountains is the Forestry Commission site just a short distance from the village.

Here you really are in the heart of Snowdonia, reached by the most direct route along the A4085 from Caernarvon. Before heading for the high country, though, take time to wander through historic Caernarvon and visit the castle, one of the finest in Great Britain. Erection of the fortress was begun by Edward I in 1283, and completed by his son. Just outside the town on the road to Beddgelert is the site of the original Roman military settlement, Segontium.

As a first taste of the high country, it would be hard to improve on the fairly gentle ascent of Moel Hebog, The Hill of the Hawk, one of the most impressive of a great half-circle of peaks, especially when seen from the north-east. The track to the 2566-foot summit begins at the village of Beddgelert and culminates in what are arguably some of the best views in the whole of the National Park.

It was on these precipitous slopes that Owen Glendower, the Welsh hero of old, hid when pursued by the English. Moel Siabod (2860 feet) is another peak in the Hebog range; it is easily ascended from Capel Curig and gives splendid views of the mountains of Snowdonia and of the Irish Sea. The beautiful Lledr Valley, of interest to both the geologist and the botanist, is close by.

Beddgelert Forest stretches away from the picturesque village, northwards towards Caernarvon. It touches upon the foot of Snowdon where the Rhyd-ddu and Beddgelert tracks begin their tortuous and spectacular 3-mile ascent to the summit. More extensive still is Gwydyr Forest which radiates in huge sweeps from Betws-y-Coed, covering the broad vale of the River Conwy north to Llanrwst and along the Llugwy Valley west of Betws-y-Coed. In between, the variety of trees softens the landscape around the Swallow Falls and other beauty spots like the Miners' Bridge and the lakes of Llynau Mymbyr near Capel Curig.

The road which connects Beddgelert with Capel Curig (A498 and A4086) is an alluring stretch, with Moel Siabod rising on one side, Snowdon and the Glyders on the other. In between are the shining waters of Llyn Dinas and Llyn Gwynant and the Pen-y-Gwryd Hotel, the training headquarters of the British team that was first to climb Mount Everest in 1953. This only emphasizes

Right Y Wyddfa (Snowdon) seen from across the lovely Llyn Padarn.

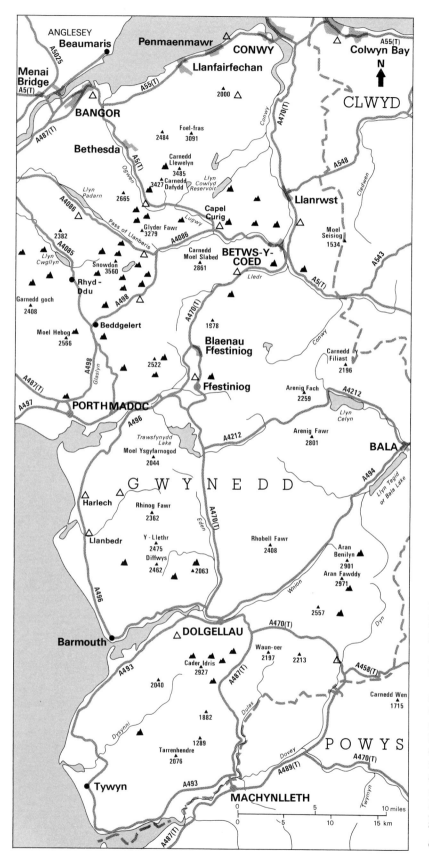

the obvious attraction of these mountain ranges for the serious climber. One challenge is presented by the twin peaks of Rhinog Fawr and Rhinog Fach, separated by a wild, 1255-foot pass. Set in a remote part beyond the village of Llanbedr, between Harlech and Barmouth, they should only be attempted by the experienced.

At Pen-y-Gwryd, at the foot of the famous Llanberis Pass, there are two prime choices for the high-country explorer, depending on which delight he wishes to sample first, Snowdon or the Glyders. For the latter, the usual approach route is from Llyn Ogwen, alongside the A5, north-west of Capel Curig. The track winds via Llyn Idwal and the conspicuous Idwal Slabs; this is the prelude to some of the most jagged and splintered summit peaks in Britain, including much-climbed Tryfan (3010 feet), the chaotic rock debris of Glyder Fach (3262 feet), and The Castle of the Winds, atop the three-peak crest of Glyder Fawr (3279 feet). The twin summits of the Glyders provide the roughest going in Wales and are the territory of only experienced climbers and the strongest hill-walkers.

From these savage and wind-swept granite heights, the eye is pulled constantly south-west across the Llanberis Pass to where the mighty Snowdon rises. And it is from the top of the Pass, beside the Pen-y-Pass youth hostel, that most first-timers make their acquaintance with Y Wyddfa, at 3560 feet the highest mountain in England and Wales.

While it has this distinction, its summit is not difficult to reach. In fact, Snowdon is one of the easiest of mountains to ascend, and there are several routes including the famous and heavily used rack-railway. The two most popular footpaths begin from the car park at Pen-y-Pass, itself 1170 feet above sea level. These summit routes are known respectively as the Miners' Track and the Pyg (or P.Y.G.) Track.

The former is easy and quite gradual at first, crossing Llyn Llydaw via the Causeway and from there along the lake edge to join the Pyg Track above Glaslyn. The latter, though not quite so well defined, is obvious enough, and at the same time more direct and more interesting. 'Pyg' is claimed to be the abbreviation of the name of the Pen-y-Gwryd Hotel, presumably to commemorate the part played in the construction of the Track by climbers from that headquarters.

Although literally millions have stood on Snowdon's summit since the first recorded climb in 1639, this in no way detracts from the majesty of the great Horseshoe ridge, especially in winter when there are few other walkers and the tops are snow-capped. It is a mountain which, while forming the very roof of Wales, is at once eminently suitable for the novice hill-walker.

Not so the higher reaches of the Carneddau range which effectively walls in the entire area of north-eastern Snowdonia. A massive series of plateaux rather than individual peaks characterize this region. For tentative exploration there is a footpath which leads from Capel Curig to the beautifully situated Llyn Crafnant reservoir. Exploring the loftier faces is a much sterner pursuit, however. It is a long and arduous trek to the summit of Llewelyn, for example, central and highest of the Carnedds at 3484 feet. The recognized route lies due north of Llyn Ogwen, but there are many false crests and tricky faces before the crest is reached. This is a ridge walk essentially for the experienced.

For the majority of hill-walkers, even the fittest and strongest, a day spent on the Carnedds means a day at full physical stretch. All the more astounding, then, is the record of Joss Naylor, Lake District farmer and champion fell-runner, who holds the record for the Welsh Fourteen Peaks: 22 miles of ascent and descent over 14 peaks all in excess of 3000 feet, from the summit of Snowdon to the top of Foel Fras at the northern end of the Carnedds in a time of 4 hours 46 minutes. To complete the route at all, irrespective of time taken, is still a commendable achievement.

Below The path along the ridge of Crib Goch is one of the wildest and most arduous approach routes to the summit of Snowdon.

Southern Snowdonia

The southern part of the National Park, below the coastal resort of Barmouth, is dominated by mighty Cader Idris, Arthur's Chair, one of another spectacular mountain group rising to nearly 3000 feet. The starting-point for most ascents of this range is Dolgellau.

From the narrow summit ridge, Pen-y-Gader, it is possible to see as far as Ireland on a clear day, while the small glacial lake, Llyn-y-Gader, glitters below. The trek to the summit is hard going in places, either via the old Pony Track or the Foxes' Path. Both start alongside the lane a couple of miles south-west of Dolgellau. There is a lot of scree and some modest scrambling is involved on the 3-mile ascent, especially on the Foxes' Path. The peak of Cader Idris itself rises to 2927 feet.

Some of the steeper faces of this group are regularly tackled by climbers, who find the grades severe enough to satisfy even the most experienced. Yet even hill-walking calls for tenacity in places, and Cader Idris, like Snowdon or any of the Welsh peaks over 2000 feet, should never be treated lightly. There are a variety of touring-parks and camping-grounds around Barmouth and Dolgellau, any of which would be a good base from which to explore the Cader Idris range.

Those heading directly for southern Snowdonia usually choose the A494 via Lake Bala and Dolgellau. This is understandable, as Lake Bala is an acknowledged hill-walking centre of the gentler kind, while Dolgellau lies almost in the shadow of Cader Idris. As an alternative, however, try the route from Betws-y-Coed both for its scenic variety and for its quintessential Welshness. The A470 is a beautiful road, at first following the steep wooded valley alongside the river Lledr and then climbing to traverse wild open moorland before descending to Blaenau Ffestiniog where the old slate mines are a popular tourist attraction.

For a most pleasant touring base, continue on the A487 towards Porthmadog and the village of Penrhyndeudraeth. One mile east is Can-y-Cefn Farm where there is a camping-ground which offers unparalleled views. Three local attractions (quite apart from the variety of hill-tracks) are the Ffestiniog Mountain Railway, Portmeirion, the Italianate fantasy village, and Harlech Castle.

Left Barmouth Estuary at the southern end of the National Park. This is an ideal centre for excursions to the southern ranges, crowned by Cader Idris.

The north-eastern region

In contrast to the far west of North Wales, the eastern perimeter offers a fine if relatively little-visited mountain range, the Clwydians, which dominate the landscape between Llangollen and Prestatyn. Here, for the hill-walker, Offa's Dyke Path is the prime pedestrian route, with the stretch between Llandegla and Bodfari being one of the most impressive.

Stamina is called upon once more to traverse this section, but the reward is well worth the effort expended. It involves some seventeen miles of successive hill-top going, broken by great stretches of open high country, forestry plantations, and a number of Iron Age hill forts. There are splendid panoramas right across Snowdonia on a clear day, before the Path eventually descends to the river Wheeler and Bodfari, a village some three miles west of Denbigh.

A short and memorable glimpse of these lovely hills can be gained by following the Moel Fammau Trail. To get there, take the A494 east of Ruthin, turn north on to the B5429, then fork right to the Forestry Commission car park. From here there is a quite challenging waymarked path mainly through forest at first, then over moorland tops to the 1820-foot summit of Moel Fammau (highest of the Clwydians) and the Jubilee Tower of George III erected – coincidentally or not – in 1820.

Right Of all the Welsh mountains, Cader Idris is second only to Snowdon in popularity. Its long ridge rises to 2927 feet.

The Lleyn Peninsula and the Isle of Anglesey

Although Snowdonia encompasses most of the dramatic high country of North Wales, there are also areas outside the National Park with strong appeal for those seeking less-trodden paths. The Lleyn Peninsula in the far north-west is one, being just sufficiently far off the tourist-track to retain an intriguing remoteness. Within the area are two cliff-top stretches that to me epitomize the wild grandeur that once enveloped the entire Principality.

Porth Dinlleyn Bay, some eight miles north-west of Pwllheli on Lleyn's western seaboard, is the first. Located in the protective curve of a splendid promontory, there is an easy footpath route to this remote beach hamlet from nearby Morfa Nefyn, and Nefyn itself, now one of the most attractive little resorts in North Wales. There is a beach and low cliff-path winding to the headland point passing through Porth Dinlleyn, one of the very few hamlets in the British Isles with no made-up roads. There is an Iron Age settlement site above the hamlet. At the southern tip of Lleyn is Hell's Mouth, or Porth Neigwl, one of the few genuine storm beaches in Britain, fully exposed to the Atlantic gales.

Above Lleyn lies Anglesey which, despite its rather dull landscape, particularly in comparison with Snowdonia, does have a few high spots around the coast. The most impressive is not really on Anglesey at all, but on Holy Island off the west coast which is connected to Anglesey by a causeway. South Stack cliffs and the lighthouse point of Holyhead Mountain are worthy of exploration, if only for the distant views of the Isle of Man, the Cumbrian hills, the mountains of County Down, and the full length of the Snowdonian range. There is in fact much more to stimulate the walker. The cliff-path itself is ruggedly exciting, especially the 400-odd rock steps that link South Stack to the main island, and the setting of the lighthouse, on its spume-swept rock platform.

You tread here in ancient footsteps, for this was yet another favoured landfall of the early Irish Christians and other, less friendly, travellers. The plateau of nearby Holyhead Mountain (a modest 710 feet, but Anglesey's loftiest landmass) was once a defensive bastion against hostile invaders. Today it is tranquil enough to attract shy sea-brids like the Fulmar, which now nest confidently along the rugged headland.

Left The gloomy vale of Nant Gwytheyrn, Vortigern's Valley, in the Lleyn Peninsula. It owes its name to the legend that Vortigern fled here after betraying his country to the Saxons.

Ordnance Survey maps: 114, 115, 116, 117, 123, 124, 125, 135

The West Country

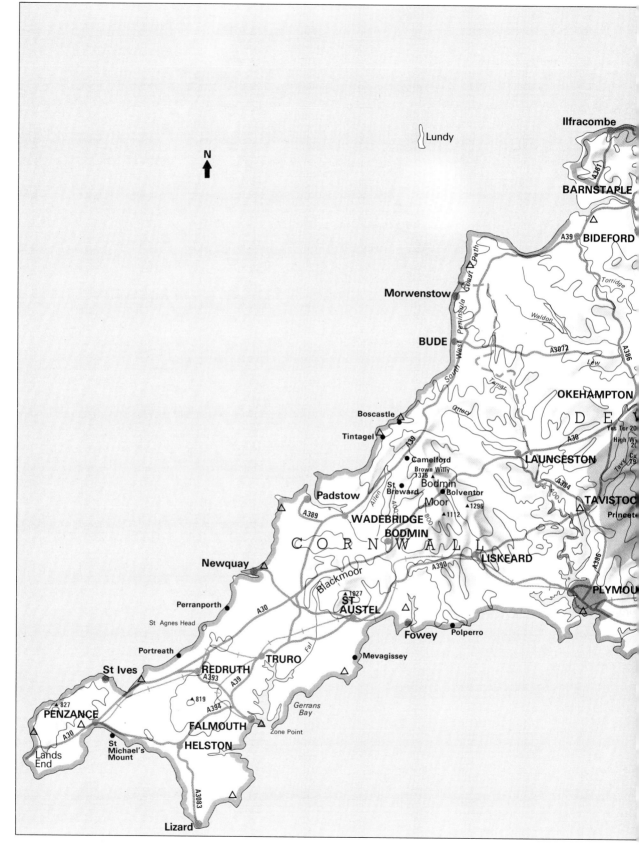

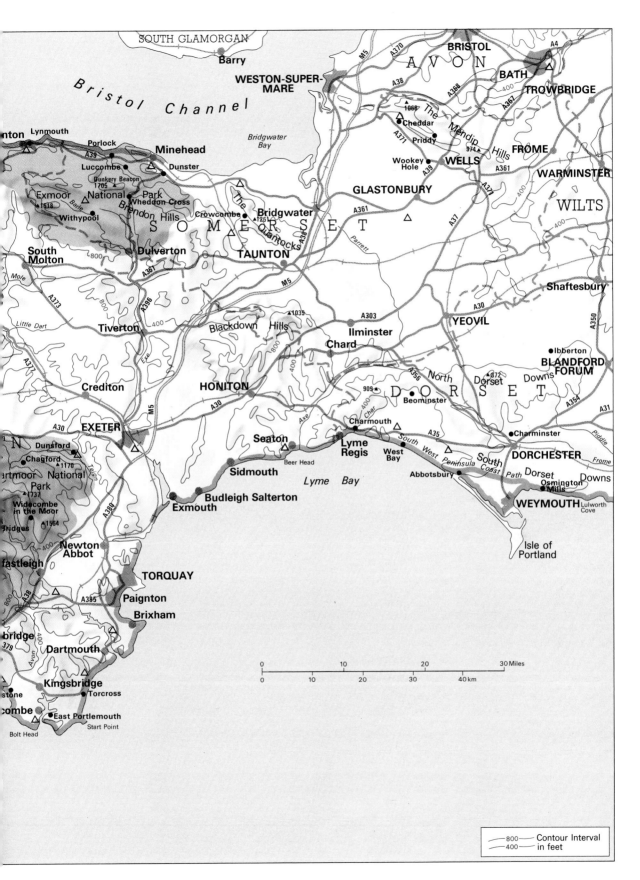

SOUTH GLAMORGAN

Barry

WESTON-SUPER-
MARE

Bristol Channel

Bridgwater Bay

BRISTOL

A V O N

BATH

TROWBRIDGE

1068

The

Mendip

Hills

FROME

Cheddar

Priddy

A371

Wookey
Hole

974

WELLS

WARMINSTER

Lynmouth

Porlock

Minehead

Dunster

A39

Luccombe

Dunkery Beacon
1705

Wheddon Cross

Exmoor

1618

National Park

Withypool

Brendon Hills

Crowcombe

Bridgwater

The Quantocks

1251

GLASTONBURY

A361

Parrett

A37

A361

FROME

A361

A367

A38

A370

M5

A368

400

A4

WILTS

South
Molton

Dulverton

TAUNTON

Shaftesbury

800

A361

A396

M5

A30

A350

Mole

YEOVIL

A371

A30

A373

Little Dart

Tiverton

800

400

1035

Blackdown Hills

Ilminster

Chard

800

Ibberton

BLANDFORD
FORUM

A30

400

Exe

A377

Crediton

HONITON

A30

M5

Axe

909

Char

D O R S E T

Beominster

872

Dorset Downs

A354

A31

Teign

Dunsford

Chagford

1170

EXETER

A30

Charmouth

Seaton

Lyme Regis

West
Bay

North

Dorset

A356

A35

Charminster

DORCHESTER

Dartmoor

National

Park

1737

Widecombe
in the Moor

1564

Bridges

Beer Head

Sidmouth

Lyme Bay

South West Peninsula

South
Coast

Path

Dorset Downs

Piddle

Frome

400

A380

Newton
Abbot

Budleigh Salterton

Exmouth

Abbotsbury

Osmington
Mills

WEYMOUTH

Lulworth
Cove

A38

A382

TORQUAY

Paignton

A385

Isle of
Portland

Brixham

bridge

379

Dartmouth

Avon

Kingsbridge

Torcross

stone

combe

East Portlemouth

Start Point

Bolt Head

0		10		20		30 Miles

0   10   20   30   40 km

800 —— Contour Interval
400 —— in feet

65

Somerset and Devon

Cheddar Gorge

Ask anyone who has visited the West Country what he remembers best, and he will very probably pick out Cheddar Gorge. Since the early days of this century it has become an increasingly popular target of ever-growing numbers of visitors, eager to marvel at this awe-inspiring natural phenomenon. Yet despite the visitors who throng the lower approaches in the summer, the Gorge still retains its timeless grandeur. Fortunately, for those active and curious enough to want a wider view, the crowds are concentrated, and with only little effort it is possible to escape for high ground that is as exhilarating in reality as suggested in any photograph.

An immediate, irresistible escape route is up Jacob's Ladder amid the show-caves, cheese shops, and souvenir sellers at the foot of the Gorge. If you can complete the stair climb without pausing for breath you are in pretty fair physical condition. You can climb more steps to the top of the observation tower if you feel so inclined, but the natural and progressive splendour of the Gorge is only revealed to the walker who takes the cliff-top path north-east towards Black Rock Gate. This is one of the most impressive 1½ miles of footpath in south-west Britain – and, of course, is just as exciting in the opposite direction.

Horseshoe Bend, the Pinnacles, and Lion Rock are laid out below like an unfolding relief map. The cliff face below the path is considered one of the finest limestone climbs in the country. Here is the high realm of the jackdaw, a remarkable abundance of wild flowers, and yet another landscape as fascinating and varied as it is ancient.

Honey-combed with caves, these cliffs which tower up to a height of 450 feet have been inhabited by man since the very dawn of history. At Gough's, the premier show-cave at the foot of the Gorge, a Neolithic skeleton was unearthed some years ago. Certainly Stone Age man knew the caves well, according to archaeological evidence. Even these may have been relative late-comers to what was patently a congenial climatic area for shelter and food-gathering, as the many prehistoric burial mounds on the Mendip uplands indicate.

Right Wide and exhilarating views over Cheddar Gorge await the walker who follows the paths to the top of the cliffs.

The Mendip Hills

The elevation of the Mendips is only modest (the highest spot is the summit of Black Down, north-east of Cheddar, 1067 feet), but it is the formation of the landscape folds that makes the Hills visually exciting. A walk through the dramatic Ebbor Gorge near Priddy will serve as one example for many.

A mile or so from the gracious cathedral city of Wells there is a memorial to Sir Winston Churchill alongside the A371 and the start of a grand waymarked walk, at first through thick woods, then dog-legging for a marvellous view of a gorge which, in its way, is every bit as impressive as its Cheddar counterpart. Ebbor Gorge covers over a hundred acres which are now a nature reserve owned by the National Trust. Some of the rich archaeological finds made in the area are on display at Wells Museum.

Wookey Hole Caves just to the north are worth a visit, if only to see the stage-lit stalactites and stalagmites, especially the Witch of Wookey stalagmite. Here over hundreds of millions of years the river Axe has eroded the limestone, revealing the remains of mammoths, sabre-toothed tigers, and early Man.

There are a number of well-placed camping-grounds in the area. The one at Mendip Heights, just north-west of the village, offers direct footpath access to a choice of rock-scrambling faces, pot-holes, and the prehistoric burial mounds of Nine Barrows.

The Quantocks

South-west from the Mendips, between Bridgwater Bay and the Vale of Taunton, lie the romantically named Quantocks, covering 400-million-year-old bed-rock of lime, sandstone, and slate grits. Small as hill ranges go – around 50 square miles – they are a relative backwater haven of combes and bracken-carpetted slopes. Will's Neck, south-east of Crowcombe, is the highest point, rising to 1260 feet above sea level. Never broader than some four miles, the 12-mile walk along the ridge is both easy and very pleasant. Crowcombe is a good centre from which to make shorter excursions, and the Quantock Forest Trail is located midway between here and Bridge. From the pretty hamlets of East Quantoxhead or Nether Stowey, at Seven Wells there is a fine circular hill-route inland, part of it along a prehistoric track-way. Another route runs towards the coast to the cliffs and ruins of Kilve Priory, founded in the fourteenth century and once, according to the guide book, a haunt of smugglers.

This part of Somerset was much loved by Coleridge and Wordsworth; Coleridge wrote *The Ancient Mariner* at Nether Stowey. At the western edge of the Quantocks, where the landscape levels out briefly, before rising again as the Brendon Hills, there is a skein of old-world farming villages including Williton, Monksilver, Stogumber, and Wiveliscombe.

Below The Quantocks near St Andrews, a region of softly rolling hills enfolding deep green valleys.

Exmoor National Park

So to Exmoor National Park which contains some of the most beautiful – and most visited – coastal and inland heights in the country. Holiday crowds need be no part of the hill-walker's scene, however, for though the park may be small the scenery is on the grand scale. Indeed it might be said that Exmoor was created for the delight and enjoyment of the walker.

The best footpath routes follow the steep, sometimes precipitous, wooded slopes of the water-courses that snake down from the wind-swept heights to form the rivers Exe, Barle, Mole and the East and West Lyn. Yet most of the rivers flow more gently, particularly south of Dunkery Beacon. At 1705 feet, the highest point in the Park, the Beacon dominates the central heights and is an obvious target for keen hill-walkers. There is a waymarked route from Wheddon Cross on the A396 between Dunster and Dulverton; it is strenuous going across windy terrain, but the views are invigorating. Another dramatic path leads from Luccombe, seawards of the rounded hill, and eventually to Porlock.

For a taste of pastoral Somerset, make for Withypool in the south-west corner of the Park and take the footpath to Tarr Steps, one of the best-preserved ancient clapper bridges in England. The path runs for almost the whole of its 4 miles along the banks of the Barle and takes in some gentle hill-climbing on the way. It is a secluded stretch, where you may catch the odd sight of red deer or even otters.

It is Exmoor's coast that carries the most traffic, both motorized and pedestrian. It is the walker who has the advantage, though, as by far the best way to get the most from this landscape is to walk a section of the South-West Peninsula Coast Path.

From Minehead, for instance, the ascent westwards quickly steepens to cross North Hill, then follows some lovely high-level walking towards Selworthy Beacon where the viewpoint, at 1012 feet above sea level, is a rewarding objective. Another route, much favoured since there is usually easy car parking at Porlock Weir, climbs alongside Yearnor Wood then continues on cliff-tops high above the sea. Culbone is one magnet on this walk, the tiniest church in England, reachable only by footpath and tucked away in a glade.

This route eventually emerges at County Gate on the A39 (the Somerset-

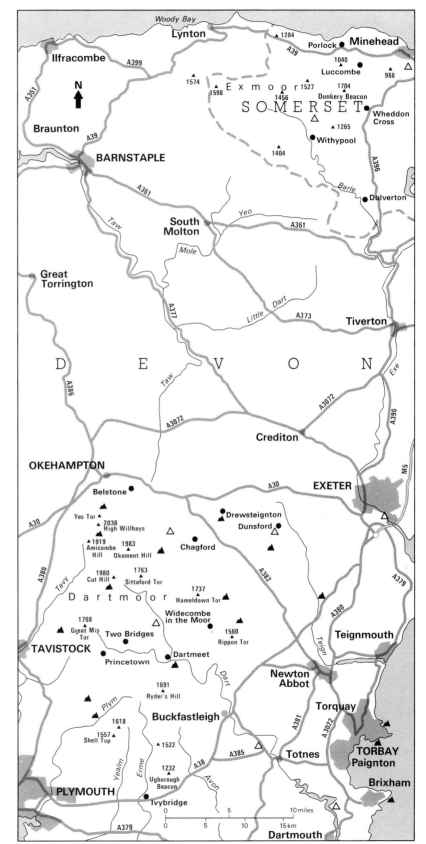

Devon border) where there is a large car park and information centre. Yet another classic walk follows immediately: across Countisbury Common, before plummeting downwards to sea level and Lynmouth. Given good weather, this is a hike to set the blood tingling. There is a youth hostel at Lynton, Lynmouth's twin town perched on top of the cliffs, and a well-run camping-ground at nearby Lynbridge. There is a fine walk direct from here over the Cleave to Watersmeet. The views of Lynmouth far below as the Path emerges from the wooded slopes are headily impressive.

West of Lynton village the Path traverses the curious Valley of Rocks, a vast arena set among fern-clad hills to the south and rocky peaks on the seaward side. On through Woody Bay, where atop The Beacon at 800 feet there was once a Roman signal station. There are some mighty ups and downs along this stretch, especially in and out of secretive Heddon's Mouth Cleave (a favoured haunt of badgers), before the Path reaches Hunter's Inn.

Although quite secluded in parts, this section of the Path is well walked, but for a stretch of switchback walking where you will find yourself alone for the most part, even in high summer, make for the village of Hartland, just inland from Hartland Point. There is a pleasant camping-ground here, a good base from which to tackle the Coast Path to the

Above On the north cliff above the spectacular Valley of Rocks near Lynmouth.

Devon-Cornwall border near Morwenstow, surely one of the most exciting stretches of our coastline.

This really is rugged and regal, with crashing Atlantic surf and flying spume assaulting the great cliffs. There is superb bathing at Welcombe Mouth, and at Marsland Mouth, which marks the Cornwall boundary, the scenery has already changed markedly from that of neighbouring Devon, the cliffs more jagged, the woodland sparse, hamlets smaller and rarer, the combes not quite so luxuriant. Cornwall is a chapter all on its own.

Dartmoor National Park

From the invigorating Atlantic coast, then, to the balmier English Channel seaboard. On the way lies Dartmoor, while dedicated walkers might even suggest a brief return to the heights of Exmoor to explore the Two Moors Way which links the two parks. This does involve some 103 miles of walking, between Lynmouth and Ivybridge, so perhaps only those with ample time and enthusiasm will be tempted. The path is hilly, still only partially waymarked, and decidedly hard going in places. The terrain includes some fine open high moorland at either end, but the middle section is mostly along river valleys and green lanes. It traverses both the National Parks from north to south, passing through much of what is still largely secret Somerset and Devon countryside. It has all the ingredients for a stimulating two-week walking holiday.

Dartmoor represents virtually the last untamed countryside in southern Britain. Friendly and welcoming when the sun shines, but forbidding, tricky, even dangerous when the mists descend from the vast granite tors that thrust skywards above lush and beautiful valleys.

Two Bridges, where two roads cross between the high moors, is the recognized centre for the car-borne visitor. A pretty enough spot certainly, but to see untamed Dartmoor you must be a walker. The pedestrian routes along footpaths and

Above Hound Tor in the centre of Dartmoor. The ruins of a Saxon longhouse were found on its eastern slopes.

back lanes from Widecombe in the Moor to Haytor Rocks, and along the ancient Abbot's Way from Buckfastleigh to Princetown, are just two possibilities.

Postbridge, near the centre of the moor, is a good starting-point for walking expeditions, with paths radiating in all directions, notably to Cut Hill. There are some army ranges in this area, though red flags are prominently displayed when firing is imminent.

Dartmeet and the vicinity of Chagford attract many visitors, but for loftier ground you have to venture into the north-eastern corner of the Park. The area south of Okehampton offers a variety of good accommodation and camping-grounds, all giving access to the most majestic of Dartmoor's high spots. The walk from Belstone, for example, around Belstone Skaigh, is a superb scene-setter.

From the village of Lydford, some seven miles north of Tavistock and overlooking the western slopes of the moor, it is not far to Yes Tor and the loftiest of them all, High Willhays (2038 feet). Also close by is Lydford Gorge and the forest trail through Lydford Forest.

If you do not wish to walk alone, you can join one of the guided walks starting from the car park below the 1490-foot Haytor Rocks. Walks are conducted under expert guidance at a very modest charge, lasting from one to six hours, and the programme operates daily throughout the summer. Similar walks start from a host of other points around the moor. This is an excellent way for novices to learn safely about Dartmoor (and indeed any wild country), away from the roads. A free schedule is available from any of the numerous Park Information Centres.

A less hectic entry route than the hard-pressed A30 is to make directly for the centre of Exeter then take the B3212 Moretonhampstead road past Steps Bridge. From there, one attractive road route leads via Dunsford and then west to Fingle Bridge near Drewsteignton. The river Teign rushes through a deep gorge here to create a striking beauty spot, popular for picnics. There are several marked footpaths.

Below The landscape of Dartmoor is one of wide variation, from bleak open moor to wooded valleys, steep green slopes, and small fields.

The South Devon Coast

Devon enjoys a reputation as the most popular holiday area in Britain, reflected in the masses of visitors who flock to the coast in the summer months. There are still parts which are less hard pressed, however, where comparative seclusion can be found, even in the high season. One is the stretch of coast between Sidmouth and the mouth of the river Exe. Sidmouth is a delightful little resort nestling between impressive red cliffs and a network of relatively empty lanes.

Walter Raleigh's birthplace is near East Budleigh, not far from the equally scenic Budleigh Salterton. Between here and Sidmouth lies the village of Otterton and from there a minor road leads to Ladram Bay where there is a well-organized and semi-secluded touring-park. Follow the Coast Path from here to Peak Hill, rising to 500 feet just west of Sidmouth, for some exciting and dramatic walking. There are splendid views in both directions from the summit, including some of the grandest red cliffs in the county and the strangely contrasting white of Beer Head to the east.

The other celebrated high-cliff stretch of Devon coast is that around Salcombe. The Coast Path runs between Thurlestone to the north-west and Torcross and Slapton Sands to the north-east, taking in Bolt Head and Start Point. There is the site of a Neolithic settlement at Bolt Tail some 400 feet above sea level. The walk from here to Bolt Head is largely across majestic open cliffs. The Path runs on the needle slivers of Sharp Tor before descending from the lofty tops through the heavily wooded slopes into Salcombe.

There is a ferry to take you from Salcombe to East Portlemouth, where you pick up the Path again to Prawle Point, the southernmost tip of Devon. Beach-walking through little Matchcombe Cove is followed by the ascent to jagged Start Point and the lighthouse. After this comes some more of the best of cliff-top walking, culminating in the long descent to Start Bay. The distinctive Slapton Sands and that angler's Mecca, Slapton Ley, are seen from an impressive memorable height as the Path approaches Torcross.

Ordnance Survey maps: 172, 180, 181, 182, 183, 191, 192, 201, 202

Left Beer Head, near Seaton. A well-defined stretch of the South-West Peninsula Coast Path winds over the towering cliffs.

Dorset

The Dorset Hills

Dorset, like many another English county, has two quite distinct upland swathes. The major swell of the hinterland runs east to west above Dorchester, from Beaminster to Blandford Forum, between Blackmoor Vale and the sea. In the centre is Cerne Abbas, distinguished by the chalk-cut figure of a club-wielding giant, of Roman or earlier origins. This is just one of many ancient landmarks that stud the Dorset Hills, often connected by faint prehistoric tracks. The most exciting is Maiden Castle, the largest Iron Age earthworks in Britain, which covers over 125 acres; it is situated a little way off the main hill ridge, some 1½ miles from Dorchester.

There was slaughter on a horrifying scale here once, when Vespasian's Roman legionaries stormed the serrated mound to conquer the Britons within. Yet the history of Maiden Castle goes back still further, some 4000 years, when it was a Stone Age stronghold.

The downland sweep of the Dorset Hills, immortalized as the setting of Thomas Hardy's novels, is also rich in more contemporary English history. There is a footpath walk over the Downs from Beaminster to Mapperton which passes the Posy Tree, under which survivors of the Bubonic Plague of 1660 gathered to pray and to collect protective herbs. While in the village of Tolpuddle stands the sycamore tree in whose shade in 1831 began the rebellion of the six farm labourers who became known as the Tolpuddle Martyrs.

Earlier evidence of Britain's wanderers is to be found in the prehistoric hill-track which forks west from alongside the B3143 a couple of miles north-east of Dorchester, and leads to Charminster along a chalk ridge dotted with ancient burial mounds. West of Charminster is the curiously shaped Eggardon Hill, formed by a land-slip; a fine path leads over the 827-foot crest, giving wide-ranging views, particularly out to sea.

For the widest panoramas along the range of the Dorset Hills, the heights between Blandford Forum and Ibberton provide the best vantage point, notably on Bulbarrow Hill where there is an Iron Age earthworks. Ibberton is a good starting-point from which to take one of the many well-marked short paths through scenic and serene uplands that remain unspoiled; across Bulbarrow Hill in one direction, to the crest of Okeford Hill in the other. The region is made up of steep hills dividing deep cups of farmland, a near-perfect mixture of nature and pastoral endeavour, punctuated by mellow old towns of golden stone like Beaminster and Blandford.

Below The rampart and ditch of Maiden Castle, the largest prehistoric earthwork in Britain.

Right From the high crest of Eggardon Hill there are fine views over land and sea.

74

The Dorset coast

The coastline of Dorset is every bit as attractive as its hinterland, though it is only quite recently that these attractions have been appreciated by holiday-makers. The coast between Lyme Regis and Lulworth Cove is now a favourite tourist venue, but the visitor who is prepared to don walking-boots and to exercise a little muscle-power can still enjoy a degree of space and freedom, even at the height of summer. This he can do by taking the designated South-West Peninsula Coast Path which extends the length of the county; these are some of the most interesting sections.

Just beyond the Devon-Dorset border, east of Lyme Regis, there is some splendid cliff-top walking over Timber Hill to Charmouth. Charmouth is a popular resort, but the Path avoids the town itself and crosses the River Char by a footbridge on the beach and then gradually begins to ascend to Golden Cap.

At an elevation of 618 feet, this is the highest point on England's south coast and the seascape panoramas are magnificent. In sunny conditions the sandstone summit shines brightly enough to be seen from across Black Down to the east, at the famous monument to Admiral Hardy. From the Cap, the Path descends steeply to the tiny hamlet of Seatown. There are several strategically situated camping-grounds in the area, at beach level or on the cliff-tops.

From this virtually unknown cove, the Path rises through an emerald-green landscape that stretches invitingly in the direction of Eype Mouth over a whole succession of round-topped hills. It passes Doghouse Hill, through the ravine-like Eype Mouth, and then drops down to West Bay which still remains a working port. This section is in my view one of the most beautiful in the 515-mile Peninsula Path route.

Beyond West Bay the Path continues at sea level through West Bexington, with Abbotsbury Swannery and Chesil Beach worthy objectives on the way. The village of Abbotsbury is itself charming, with thatched cottages and a fifteenth-century tithe barn, all that remains of the former monastery. St Catherine's Chapel stands on a hill-top near by, while just north of the village is Abbotsbury Castle, an Iron Age hill fort. There is also an inland route starting from West Bexington, across White Horse Hill.

Another particularly fine section of the Path extends east from Weymouth, revealing scenic delights above Osmington Mills, both inland and coastal. At Osmington Mills the two routes from West Bexington converge. The coastal track winds across Burning Cliff, westwards to the distinctive chalk headland of White Nothe, and on to Swyre Head. It crosses The Warren, a fine spread of headlands and hollows, then skirts Bat's Head, a sharply defined outcrop, and runs on to Durdle Door, a magnificent archway of Purbeck Limestone.

Arrive early in the morning if you can

to enjoy at least a partial solitude which this scene really demands. The next stretch will be infinitely enjoyable too, across St Oswald's Bay, where chalk and limestone strata divide (the chalk rising up to Hambury Tout, the limestone forming the cliffs), then down eventually to Lulworth Cove, an almost perfect circle of sheltered water, surrounded by cliffs except for one narrow outlet. Despite the throngs of summer tourists, Lulworth retains much of its charm. Happily, any crowds tend to thin drastically east of Lulworth and the Path remains strikingly beautiful. The area is used extensively as a firing range by the army but walkers are allowed access when the ranges are not active, and can follow the Path to Kimmeridge, at the eastern end of Worbarrow Bay.

From Kimmeridge the Path winds upwards to the dramatic stretch along the famous Kimmeridge Ledges to St Alban's (or St Aldhelm's) Head. Though well trodden and well marked,

the Path runs along massive fissured cliffs and involves negotiating a number of quite fierce ups and downs. At St Alban's Head you come upon Chapman's Pool, scooped in the rock, while out on the point stands St Alban's Chapel.

Between here and Durlston Head the Path offers yet more marvellous high spots: East Man, Dancing Ledge, Tilly Whim Caves, and Great Globe. Reaching Peveril Point at last, the landscape becomes gentler, curving east into Swanage Bay.

There is one last dramatic pocket of Dorset cliff-top before the waters of Poole Harbour are reached – the Old Harry Rocks. Located at Handfast Point, the most easterly outcrop of the Purbecks, the chalk faces here are popular with climbers – as are the limestone ledges along the Tilly Whim cliffs.

Ordnance Survey maps: 193, 194, 195

Above left The Dorset coast offers splendid high-level walking. One particularly notable stretch is along the South-West Peninsula Coast Path over the cliff-tops from the beach at Charmouth.

Above At St Aldhelm's Head the cliffs tower to nearly 400 feet, giving magnificent views along the coast.

Cornwall

The jutting granite cliffs of Cornwall's rugged seaboard on the tip of England's western peninsula are as exciting and stimulating as its hinterland is mostly disappointing and sometimes downright dull. Less than a century ago, Cornwall was considered the remotest, wildest, and most alien county in England; almost a land apart, visited by only the most intrepid of travellers.

Things are very different now, and the problem for the present-day wanderer is not so much the wilderness itself, as the lack of it, Bodmin Moor and one or two other enclaves apart. In common with Devon and Dorset, however, the county authorities have managed to stem the worst of coastal spoilation, for which we must be thankful to schemes like Operation Neptune.

The two main stretches of Cornish coast differ from each other mainly by virtue of their climates. The Atlantic side, from above Bude to Land's End, is distinctly more bracing than the cosier, more benign south-facing coast which is lapped by gentler seas. While each has its special character and appeal, the loftier sections along both seaboards have one factor in common: for the walker the going is frequently vigorous verging on tough, the landscape only varying from absorbing to stunning.

A memorable introduction will be found along the 19-mile stretch of coast between Marsland Mouth and Bude, on the North Devon-Cornwall border. This is part of the South-West Peninsula Coast Path which runs for 515 miles round the coast from Somerset to Dorset.

It is not the easiest of walking, for there is a good deal of scrambling in and out of ravines, and the Path is not always well defined and may be hidden by bracken. The tenacious walker will respond to these conditions as something of a challenge though, as the rewards are many and the charming resort of Bude is only some six miles distant. The cliffs here and all the way past Bude to Widemouth Sands are carboniferous in origin, distinguished by layers of sandstone and shale which were formed by buckling and tilting of the rock strata some 300 million years ago.

The Path becomes easier on the approach to Bude and the last couple of

Right Kynance Cove, north-west of Lizard Point, is famed for both the strange formations and rainbow colours of the serpentine rocks.

Above Near Perranporth, on the northern Cornish seaboard, the cliffs are carved into fantastic arches, both by nature and by mining.

Above right Near Botallack, on the Coast Path, an exhilarating approach route to Land's End.

miles are smooth by comparison, over superbly springy turf. Although it has become one of the most popular surf-boarding centres in the country, Bude has managed to remain largely unspoilt. Two of the quainter historic attractions are the old canal, once used to carry fertilizer beach sand to Launceston some thirty miles away; and Compass Point Tower on the Bude Haven headland, the walls of which are inscribed with the points of the compass. There is a good choice of camping-grounds, especially around Widemouth Sands.

If that section is pleasing, the next, between Boscastle and Tintagel, is considered by many to be the most beautiful coastal walk in Britain. Certainly it is one of the best along the whole of the Peninsula Path. The going is quite splendid, again partly over springy turf, the Path hugging the cliff edge, dipping into ravines, and always revealing splendid views in every direction.

Boscastle, at the convergence of the Valency and Jordan rivers, nestling between great slate cliffs on the seaward side and the steep wooded valley inland, is a superb starting-point. Seals were once harvested here, trapped in caves beneath the soaring cliffs. A mile east of Boscastle stands the isolated church of St Juliot, restored in 1870 by a young architect and budding novelist, Thomas Hardy.

Back on the Coast Path, 4 miles ahead the ruins of Tintagel Castle stand strikingly aloof on a headland almost severed from the mainland. The popular, but false, link with King Arthur makes it a favourite tourist attraction. The Castle was in fact built by the Normans in the twelfth century.

On the northern peninsula approach, known as The Island, there are fine views of the massive slate caverns on the northern side of Tintagel Cove. A number of very good short walks start from the town, including the mile-long path through the richly wooded Rocky Valley to the waterfall of St Nectan's Kieve.

South-west of the rapidly growing resort of Newquay and beyond the great

sand-dunes around Perranporth, there is the regal St Agnes Head, offering fine views. The Coast Path between here and Godrevy Point above St Ives Bay holds yet more delights for the walker. There is the near-vertical plummet to the cove of Portreath, then up again as steeply for the traverse of Reskajeage Downs. Still the grand cliffs unfold, the most spectacular the satanic Hell's Mouth, which really is awesome to behold in an angry sea.

Land's End itself may prove disappointing at first sight, not only because of the brash commercialism, but because the cliffs themselves are not particularly notable. One of the best approach routes, however, is from the Coast Path at Sennen Cove. It is only a couple of miles, but they are enough to put the walker in the right mood to appreciate the romance and atmosphere of this westernmost point of Britain.

The trippers may throng Land's End in their coach-loads, but a few steps along the Coast Path will bring the walker back into serene and rugged surroundings, the only sounds the plaintive cries of sea-birds and the thunder of the surf.

Eastwards past the development of Mount's Bay, beyond Penzance with St Michael's Mount offshore, is the stern, almost stark, Lizard Peninsula. On the approach to the southern wind-swept tip lies Kynance Cove, now largely under the protection of the National Trust. A magnificent path winds around the cove, which contains a wealth of caves, blow-holes, and strange formations of multi-coloured serpentine rock. It is a scenic feast, capped by some fiercesome jagged rocks offshore.

The view inland across the desolate Lizard Peninsula is bleak by contrast. The cliffs in this vicinity reach a height of about 180 feet; near Cadgwith there is a huge cliff chasm known as the Devil's Frying Pan.

One of the quieter corners of Cornwall in the summer months, and one of the most scenic, is the Roseland Peninsula facing Falmouth across the wide Carrick Roads. A backwater of lush green hills and a wealth of trees – fairly unusual in the county – the area is affectionately known as Cornwall in Aspic. There is a pleasant touring site near Veryan, with some interesting stretches of cliff to

explore close by, notably around Port-loe. There is good walking around Zone Point and Gerrans Bay.

It is difficult to single out individual high spots among so many, but one worthy of mention is the notorious Dodman Point – a seamen's corruption of Deadman – the massive headland above Goran Haven. This sky-scraper bluff of treacherous rocks is topped by an ancient granite cross, with a precipitous path down to Goran. Marvellous high-level walking will be found between here and Mevagissey, one of the most pleasing harbours in all Cornwall.

Polperro, a sleepy fishing village popular with tourists, has a long history as a haunt for smugglers; the notorious Excise Men were brought into existence largely to deal with the nefarious doings around Polperro in the early years of the nineteenth century. The walker can still follow some of the old contraband trails hereabouts if he cares to explore. There is splendid cliff-top walking, largely over National Trust land, especially west-wards towards Fowey, around Lantivet Bay, and Pencarrow Head. On the outskirts of Looe, renowned as a shark-fishing centre, holiday development escalates.

Bodmin Moor, Cornwall's mini-Dart-moor, is not among my personal upland favourites, even though it does boast the highest terrain in the county (Brown Willy, at 1375 feet) and its apparent bleakness and desolation frequently do reveal hidden delights. The whole area is only about 12 miles square, and the high

Above A track winding across Bodmin Moor towards Rough Tor. It is a drab landscape of rough grass and indecisive contours.

Right Rough Tor, at 1311 feet the second highest peak on the moor.

ground lies mainly in the north of the moor between Camelford and the A30.

Brown Willy can be scaled by a variety of routes, among them a footpath starting near Bolventnor. The summit is often hidden by cloud or sea-fret, as is its neighbour, Rough Tor. In clear weather, however, these heights really are quite impressive, almost mountains rather than moorland tops when seen at a distance.

A minor road runs north–south between Bolventnor and Liskeard, and from this there is footpath access to Dozmary Pool (the legendary resting-place of King Arthur's sword, Excalibur), and some wild tracks over Smallacombe Downs. Jamaica Inn, the appropriate setting for Daphne Du Maurier's novel, lies alongside this road which largely follows the banks of the river Fowey and must cover a much older track. Even in prehistoric times Bodmin must have been a pretty forbidding prospect, as there are only few relics, suprising given the dominant high ground. There is a stone circle called Stripple Stones, and an earthworks near St Breward known as King Arthur's Hall, estimated to be 4000 years old.

Ordnance Survey maps: 190, 200, 201, 203, 204

Central England

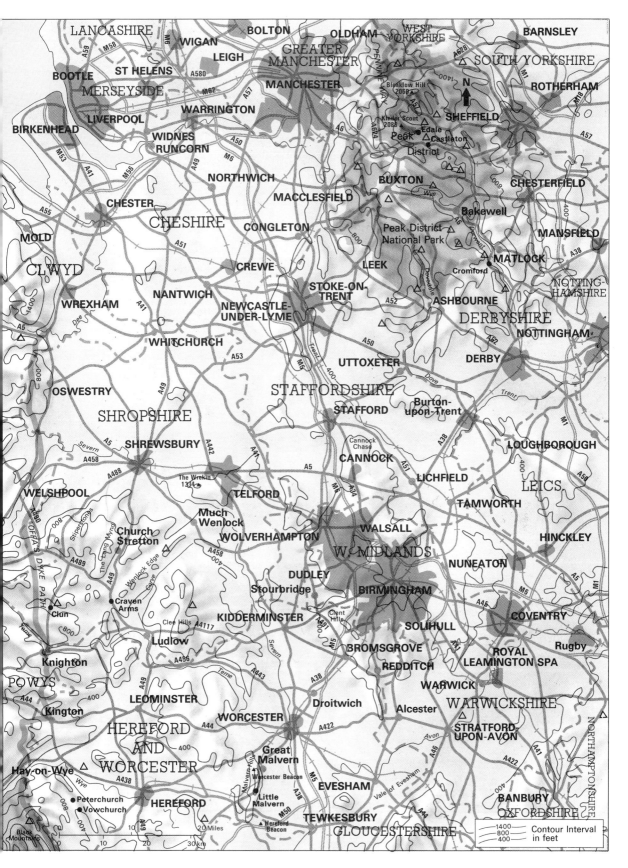

LANCASHIRE

WIGAN
BOLTON
OLDHAM
WEST YORKSHIRE
BARNSLEY

LEIGH
GREATER MANCHESTER
SOUTH YORKSHIRE

BOOTLE
ST HELENS
MANCHESTER
Bleaklow Hill 2060
ROTHERHAM

MERSEYSIDE
WARRINGTON
Kinder Scout 2088
SHEFFIELD

LIVERPOOL
WIDNES
Peak
Edale
Castleton

BIRKENHEAD
RUNCORN
District

NORTHWICH
BUXTON
CHESTERFIELD

CHESTER
MACCLESFIELD
Bakewell
MANSFIELD

CHESHIRE
CONGLETON
Peak District National Park

MOLD
Wye

CLWYD
CREWE
LEEK
MATLOCK
NOTTING-HAMSHIRE

WREXHAM
NANTWICH
STOKE-ON-TRENT
Cromford

NEWCASTLE-UNDER-LYME
ASHBOURNE
DERBYSHIRE
NOTTINGHAM

WHITCHURCH
A50
DERBY

OSWESTRY
UTTOXETER

SHROPSHIRE
STAFFORDSHIRE
Dove

SHREWSBURY
STAFFORD
Burton-upon-Trent
Trent

The Wrekin 1334
Cannock Chase
LOUGHBOROUGH

WELSHPOOL
TELFORD
CANNOCK
LEICS

Much Wenlock
LICHFIELD

Church Stretton
WOLVERHAMPTON
TAMWORTH

Craven Arms
WALSALL
HINCKLEY

Clun
DUDLEY
W. MIDLANDS
NUNEATON

Clee Hills
Stourbridge
BIRMINGHAM

Ludlow
KIDDERMINSTER
Clent Hills
SOLIHULL
COVENTRY

Knighton
BROMSGROVE
ROYAL LEAMINGTON SPA
Rugby

POWYS
LEOMINSTER
REDDITCH
WARWICK

Kington
Droitwich
Alcester
WARWICKSHIRE

HEREFORD
WORCESTER
STRATFORD-UPON-AVON

AND
Great Malvern
Avon

WORCESTER
Worcester Beacon
EVESHAM
Vale of Evesham

Hay-on-Wye
Little Malvern
BANBURY

Peterchurch
HEREFORD
Hereford Beacon
OXFORDSHIRE

Vowchurch
TEWKESBURY

Black Mountains
GLOUCESTERSHIRE

1400
800
400
Contour Interval in feet

Midlands High Country

The Black Country

Just as Londoners can escape to the green space of the Home Counties, so Britain's Second City is well endowed with open country around its perimeters. From the heart of Birmingham – 'wondrous wooded and arable', according to the Domesday Book – it is not far to Warwickshire. Although it is not hill country in the strict sense around Alcester and the Vale of Evesham, it is green and pleasant enough; while Cannock Chase, to the north in Staffordshire's Black Country, with its 28 square miles of gently undulating hills clad with heather and birch, is good training ground

for the walker with higher aspirations.

Do not think that central England is devoid of lofty heights; far from it, as the countless Midlanders who roam the Worcestershire Clent Hills will know. They rise to over a thousand feet, only a dozen miles from the city bustle; from the ridge of Walton Hill it is possible to see North Wales on a clear day. There is easy access to these tops from Clent village, just off the A491 some six miles from Bromsgrove. The quartet of standing stones on the ridge, north-east of the village, look authentic, but they are actually an eighteenth-century folly. The landscape all around, however, is totally

genuine, beautiful and very old. The estimated age of the hill rock is between 200 and 300 million years. Much of this area is now under the protection of the National Trust.

The adjacent Walton Hills are almost equally scenic, as are the woodlands of the Clatterbach Valley. Some three miles north-west lies Stourbridge in Staffordshire and from here there is more easy access to another famous viewpoint, Kinver Edge, also National Trust property. From this ridge, crowned by an Iron Age hill fort, there are wide panoramic views, claimed by many to be the finest in all Staffordshire. The whole

ridge is a natural delight of heath, and the sandstone caves of Holy Austin Rock are particularly intriguing. These 'rock houses', as they are known locally, were almost certainly inhabited by early Man, though evidence of occupation only goes back to Medieval times when some of the caves were re-structured and, later, provided with walls.

Those seeking the more elevated parts of Shakespeare Country could try Cleeve Hill in the Vale of Evesham. There is some good footpath walking from Bidford-on-Avon, especially along the south bank of the river in the direction of Bredon Hill. This particular limestone whaleback boasts two Iron Age forts on its summit. Effort is rewarded with the ascent and traverse of Cleeve Hill, which commands fine views westwards.

From the village of Bidford there is an arrow-straight stretch of Roman road, Icknield Street, or Ryknild Street, a route which probably existed even before Roman times. It leads northwards to Alcester, known to have been of Roman origin, and from there to Droitwich, called Salinae by the Romans. It is quite possible, therefore, that this was the ancient Salt Route, winding south through the Cotswolds and via the Thames Valley to London.

Above left The Clent Hills near Stourbridge. This extensive area of unspoilt countryside offers a wide range of walks for city-dwellers in central England.

Above Bredon Hill, seen here from across the river Avon, is an outlier of the Cotswolds and a notable landmark in the area, rising to 961 feet.

The Malvern Hills

Across the wide and fertile valley of the Severn, in an almost direct line from Evesham, lie the Malvern Hills, dominating a landscape once part of the ancient kingdom of Mercia. This is another of England's spectacular, if very compact, hill ranges, scarcely 10 miles in length and hardly more than a few hundred yards across for much of this distance.

The Malverns rise so abruptly from their low-lying surroundings that they make an impressive distant landmark. They were beloved of Sir Edward Elgar, who drew inspiration for much of his stirring music from these slim yet lofty hills. Birchwood, his birthplace and home, is at Lower Broadheath near Worcester and is open to visitors.

Much of the enchantment of the Malverns lies in the great variety of terrain within so small a compass and the superb views gained from the tops in good weather. Although surrounded now by busy roads, towns, and villages and walked by countless thousands, the Malverns still manage to retain a particular magic acknowledged by all who have ever enjoyed them.

Those not used to hill-walking may find the ridge path surprisingly severe in places and may wish to revive themselves in Great Malvern. Not that any excuse is needed, for the spa town, an established settlement in the eleventh century, has an attractive continental flavour, partly because of the way it is terraced on the hillside. Once the site of a Benedictine priory, its later claim to fame was the therapeutic waters of Malvern Wells, discovered in the seventeenth century.

Little Malvern, in its attractive wooded setting, was also the site of a priory (twelfth century). Although the hills extend for some distance further north, the logical starting-point for the walker is Great Malvern, which nestles snug just below the northern end of the scarp. Around the shoulder of North Hill splendid views open out across the upper Severn Valley, the obvious footpath taking the walker on to Worcestershire Beacon, the highest of the summits at 1394 feet.

An exhilarating switch-back ridge follows, with sweeping vistas to east and west, then a sharp descent to Wyche Cutting before a steep and sustained climb to Herefordshire Beacon (1174 feet). A huge Iron Age fort known as British Camp crowns this hill, and covers no less than 32 acres. The top-most mound is much later, probably dating from the eleventh and twelfth centuries.

The path continues above Malvern reservoir and past Giant's Cave and Red Earl's Dyke. Eastnor Park with its tall obelisk marks the recognized southwestern fringe of the hills, though there are two more, Ragged Stone and Cheese End, a little to the south. There is a youth hostel near Lower Wyche and a convenient camping-ground some three miles east of Great Malvern at Little Clevelode on the banks of the Severn.

Far left The Malvern Hills rise to nearly 1400 feet above the rolling countryside of Hereford and Worcester. At every season of the year they present a blaze of colour, from the fresh green of the trees in spring to the rich russet of the bracken in autumn.

Left The Worcestershire Beacon is the highest point of the Malvern Hills, rising sharply to 1394 feet. It is criss-crossed by many winding paths.

Shropshire

It is to the west of the great conurbations of the Midlands that the most exciting landscape is to be found: the high country of Shropshire. Surprisingly, it is relatively low on the list of popular tourist areas and receives only a fraction of the acclaim awarded to the West Country or the Lake District, for example.

Perhaps this is because, geographically, the area is just off the mainstream motorway routes; possibly because it is so close to Wales that the mightier mountains further west are a stronger magnet. But whatever the reason, those visitors who choose Shropshire as a touring ground are generally delighted with what they discover. Veteran hill-walkers, of course, will be well aware what Salop has to offer; they will also know that the high spots can be reached along almost empty roads for most months of the year and that base camps will be comfortably uncrowded.

The area lies roughly between Ludlow and Shrewsbury, bisected by the A49 north to south, but fortunately crossed by many attractive secondary and un-classified roads both east and west. Shrewsbury itself, historic capital of the county, nestles in a great horseshoe bend of the Severn and is rich in six-teenth-century half-timbered houses, with a noble skyline of towers and spires. It is an excellent place to visit if wet weather keeps you from the hills; there is an information centre in the town square.

It is the hills that are the real lure though, and for an initial approach full of visual delight from the south, take the A456 from Kidderminster and then the A4117 to Cleobury Mortimer. From here you enter the Heart of England, especially if you leave the main road and head along minor roads to Cleeton St Mary nestling among the Clee Hills. Here, the scene has a touch of the Yorkshire Dales, albeit in miniature, with the summit of Clee Hill, at 1531 feet, affording views from the Giant's Chair of several counties and even the Bristol Channel far to the south. Brown Clee, 4 miles to the north, is the highest of the Shropshire Hills (1790 feet).

The camping-ground at Cleeton Court Farm on the slopes of the Clee Hills provides a strategic – if somewhat spartan – base from which to explore this area. Several high-level tracks and forest trails

Left The wind-swept ridge of Wenlock Edge stretches for nearly 16 miles from Much Wenlock towards Craven Arms.

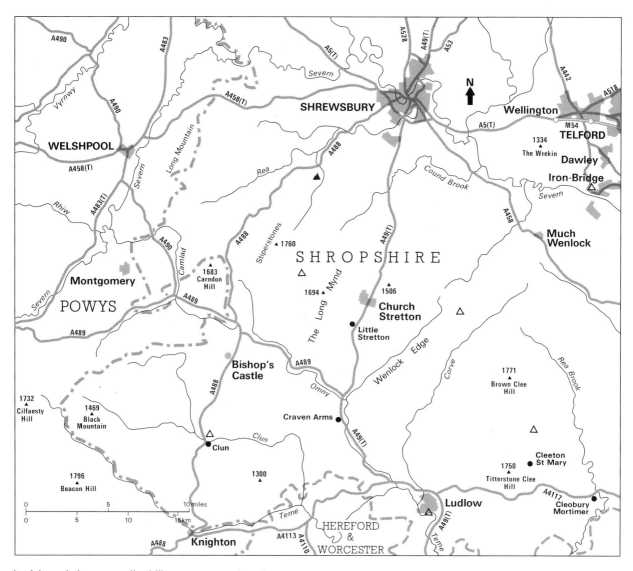

lead through the surrounding hill country. Ludlow, with its well-preserved Norman castle, set on high ground between the Teme and Corve rivers, is just 10 miles away.

North-west of Ludlow, notably around Craven Arms (known as the Crossroads of South Salop), there are a good number of touring sites, with a few strategic pitches off the B4368 between Craven Arms and Clun. There is a choice of footpath walks from here, either high level, along the adjacent hill flanks, or along the valley floor through farmland and woods.

Clun, which lends its name to a breed of sheep, is a charming little town with a turbulent history as the site of confrontation between opposing armies from the time of the Roman invasion. For an eagle's-eye view of the impressive ruined castle, climb the steep hill around the back of the church.

From Clun, it is but a few miles west to a magnificent stretch of Offa's Dyke Path. Between Knighton and Welshpool, at the foot of Long Mountain, is the longest, almost unbroken, stretch of the ancient Dyke on the entire footpath. One of the finest views of the Dyke is to be had from the summit of Llanfair Hill in the heart of the Clun Hills; at 1400 feet, this is the highest point of the earthworks. The Path is well defined, leading across the partly wooded hills.

Of all the ranges in the Shropshire Hills, there is one which is probably known to most walkers who have visited the county. This is The Long Mynd, one of the most distinctly shaped moorland plateaux in all Britain, gouged by deep valleys which contribute to an illusion of

over-all heights much greater than the actual 1700 feet.

The Long Mynd is just one hill complex in the Shropshire range; to the north-west lie the more austere Stiperstones, and the lush, wooded high country of Wenlock Edge to the south-east. You could hardly find a trio of more contrasting hill scenery in such a small area, and it is this factor which makes the terrain so fascinating to explore.

For close encounters with The Long Mynd and the Stiperstones, turn north off the A489 below the southern scarp of the Mynd at the village of Eaton, and take the minor road to Wentnor, where there is a pleasant and convenient touring site. The splintered limestone crags of the Stiperstones stand out to the north-west. Rising to 1700 feet, these are as rugged as any in central England. There

is a path along the summit ridge which extends for nearly three miles. The highest and most impressive of the rock formations is known as the Devil's Chair.

Little Stretton, just south of Church Stretton, is a good base from which to ascend The Long Mynd ridge. A good choice of footpaths lead direct from the valley to the summit. A few miles of fairly stiff ascent bring you to the top of the plateau at 1695 feet. The effort involved, however, is amply rewarded by the views from the summit, particularly of the Stiperstones.

East of The Long Mynd, along the scenic B4371, is Much Wenlock, an ancient town with Saxon origins. The Elizabethan Guildhall and the ruins of the Medieval priory are only two of its many attractions, not to mention Wenlock Edge itself, which runs for 16

unbroken miles south-west of the town all the way to Craven Arms. There is good access to the Edge from Much Wenlock, or from the two minor roads at the northern end of the scarp.

North of Much Wenlock, beyond Iron Bridge Gorge and the river Severn, stands The Wrekin, immortalized in A.E. Housman's *Shropshire Lad*. Divided from the main hill ranges, it stands out distinctively above the surrounding lowland, particularly when viewed from south of the Severn. While not the highest of the Shropshire Hills, it epitomizes all that is naturally beautiful within the county and holds a special place in the heart of every Salopian.

Ordnance Survey maps: 126, 127, 128, 137, 138, 139, 140, 150, 151

Above From the top of the plateau of The Long Mynd panoramic views open out over the Shropshire countryside.

The Peak District National Park

In 1951 the Peak District was designated National Park, the first area of outstanding, unspoiled natural beauty in Britain to receive this title. The most significant result of this far-sighted official act was to protect and preserve a vital green lung between Sheffield and Manchester from the danger of further encroachment of urban development.

I can well remember tramping and camping over this vast spread of marvellous hill country in the early 1950s when the pursuit was still confined to a relatively small minority of enthusiasts. At that time, wandering off the beaten track was likely to incur the wrath of irate landowners, though the serious walker ready to defend established rights of way did not let this deter him.

The aim behind the concept of the National Parks was to provide free access for all to the natural heritage of the countryside. Thirty years later, it can be said without hesitation that this has been achieved. Today the visitor can cross the boundaries of ten National Parks in England and Wales, secure in the knowledge that most, if not all, the natural and man-made attractions will be freely available for enjoyment. This is particularly important for the outdoor enthusiast, who is now only restricted by a number of standard by-laws.

Below One stretch of the rich and varied landscape of the National Park.

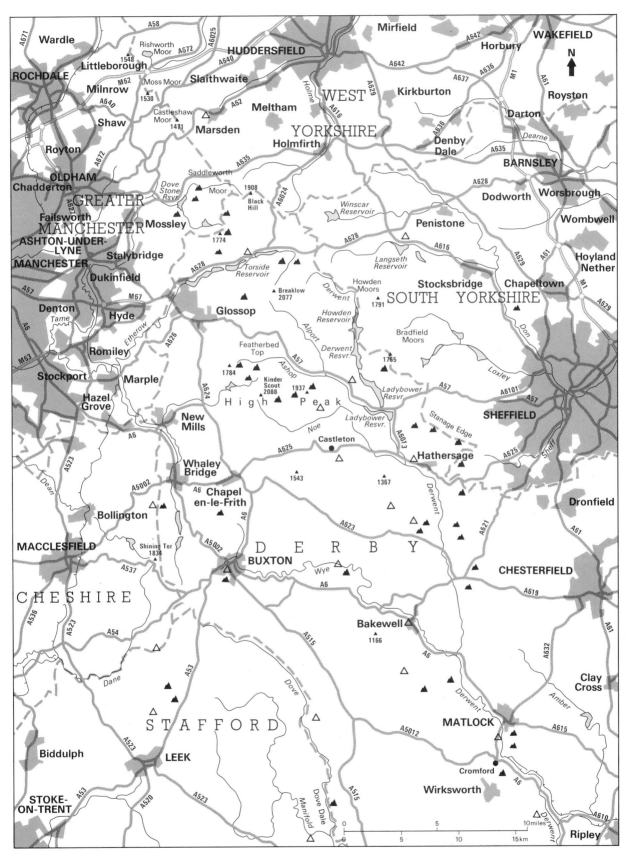

Only the veterans among the outdoor fraternity can appreciate to the full this enlightened attitude, especially those who make repeated visits. For the Peak District is so richly varied that no matter how many times you scale the hill paths, some new and interesting aspect of the landscape will be revealed. This is hardly surprising when you consider that the Park covers some 500 square miles of Derbyshire, Staffordshire, Cheshire, Greater Manchester, and West and South Yorkshire.

The Park contains two quite distinct landscapes which together form a vast upland spread. The horseshoe of gritstone moorland enclosing the central limestone plateau is the Dark Peak, which takes its name from the coloration of the mixture of gritstone, heather, and bracken. This stern stretch of country lies roughly north of an imaginary line between Macclesfield in the west and Sheffield in the east. The terrain below

this line to Ashbourne at the southern extreme is known as the White Peak, named for the grey-white limestone outcrops which stand out against the lighter greens of pasture and meadow.

The Dark Peak is really rugged high country, crowned by the brooding trio of Kinder Scout, Bleaklow, and Black Hill. Rough, tough, and exciting to traverse on foot, this is a landscape for the experienced hill-walker and certainly no place for the novice in winter. Enthusiasts come in all seasons to climb on the gritstone edges of Stanage, Curbar, and Froggatt, and bog-trotting the peat wastes of Kinder and Bleaklow is another rewarding, if strenuous, popular pursuit. It is through these wild peat moors that the Pennine Way, Britain's most romantic long-distance footpath, winds on its long way from Edale to the far-off Scottish border.

Although the White Peak is rather more gentle, it should not be under-

Above Kinder Scout (2088 feet) is one of the major heights in the Dark Peak.

Right Mam Tor, the site of an extensive Iron Age camp, separates Edale from the Hope Valley.

estimated. For make no mistake, this is still rugged plateau country, though crisscrossed by friendlier wooded valleys fed by four beautiful rivers, Derwent, Dove, Wye, and Manifold.

A good base from which to see both the 'light' and the 'dark' sides of the Park is Castleton, situated almost at the centre, about eight miles north-east of Buxton. There is a good choice of accommodation in the area, including touring sites and a youth hostel, to cater for the large numbers of visitors. One particular attraction is the local caverns, of which the Blue John Caverns are the most well known for their distinctive, and unique, stone.

A mile or so west of Castleton there is a spectacular ravine, Winnats Pass. A number of tracks and footpaths lead to the summit which offers splendid views across miles of rolling limestone countryside. Beneath the Pass lies Speedwell Cavern where lead was mined in the eighteenth century. There is a fine 5-mile round walk from Castleton up through the Pass and on to the summit of Mam Tor, which is known as Shivering Mountain because of the landslides which regularly occur.

No visit to Castleton could be complete without a climb to view the ruins of the Norman Peveril Castle, setting of Sir Walter Scott's novel, *Peveril of the Peak*. Standing high above the village, the Castle is protected on three sides by huge, natural bluffs, while the fourth is dominated by a great wall, still superbly preserved. The view from the keep is sufficient reward for the sharp, stiff climb to the top.

North of Castleton and the Hope Valley lies Edale, the celebrated and often crowded start of the Pennine Way Path, where there is always a faint tang of excitement in the air. Even if there is no personal ambition to complete the 250-mile marathon, the departure of the determined walkers is infectious, their enthusiasm often vicariously enjoyed by lesser mortals.

There are several touring sites in and around the village, together with a youth hostel and an excellent information centre, Fieldhead. The only route north from Edale, appropriately, is a pedestrian one up the Pennine Way. Edale now boasts a large car park and is still served by British Rail, both invaluable assets for those who intend walking the whole or part of the Pennine Way.

For a sample of the Way, either of the two routes to the heights of Kinder Scout should make a memorable impression on the first-time visitor. The main path –

the classic start, one might say – starts at the northern end of the village and winds snake-like up Grindsbrook, becoming progressively more rugged and involving some scrambling to get over the lip of the plateau. At once the walker is in a true wilderness of deep peat hags where map and compass will be constantly at hand.

The alternative path, which is easier and thus known as the bad weather route, is via Jacob's Ladder, west of Crowden Brook. Both routes then join and continue to Kinder Downfall, a spectacular waterfall when in spate, rushing to replenish Kinder reservoir far below. This area should not be tackled without appropriate hill-walking gear, nor should you go out alone if the weather is doubtful. After all, this is the ultimate challenge for long-distance walkers in Britain and the start, like much of the remainder, is tough, rugged, and strenuous.

Kinder itself, at an elevation of over 2000 feet, is just one of a succession of wind-swept and, at times, quite isolated peaks, amid vast tracts of peat and heather. Rather intimidating for the novice, it becomes increasingly magnetic with familiarity. It is also wildly beautiful in its way, and provides the dedicated walker with a unique sense of fulfilment among terrain that has remained almost unchanged for countless centuries. On its progress north, the Way passes through other, equally grand country, but for those who wish to soak up some of the essential atmosphere of the path, there is no better centre than Edale.

There is further interesting – if somewhat less spectacular and strenuous – hill-walking at the southern end of the Park, just north of Ashbourne, an ancient market town and gateway to Dovedale. I may have said that this countryside is less spectacular than the Dark Peak, but perhaps I should have said less stern. It is not for nothing that Dovedale has been

Left Chee Dale offers excellent walking by the river Wye and all grades of rock-climbing on its limestone outcrops.

Right Dovedale, which forms the boundary between Staffordshire and Derbyshire, is a narrow ravine whose massive sides have been carved and weathered into fantastic shapes. Walkers and climbers are drawn in ever-growing numbers to this 'Little Switzerland'.

Far right A well-tramped footpath follows the course of the Dove through the magnificent scenery of the dale.

dubbed Little Switzerland, for tramping the edge of the Dove between the walls of the gorge leads through scenery with a distinctly Alpine character. Every strangely shaped pinnacle and outcrop has a name, like the Twelve Apostles or Lovers' Leap, and there is an abundance of caves, of which Dove Holes is the grandest and best known.

The village of Ilam is a good starting-point from which to explore both Dovedale and the Manifold Valley which runs parallel and slightly west in the county of Staffordshire. The Manifold rewards the walker at Beeston Tor, a truly massive scarp, honey-combed with caves. Animal remains and fragments of pottery have been found in the caves, indicating that they were once inhabited by man. There is a superb vista of the Upper Manifold from the entrance of Thor's Cave, further up the valley.

Just east of Dovedale, the Tissington Trail traverses a striking landscape of dry-stone walls and steep-sided dales.

The Trail originated from a project undertaken by the authorities of the Peak Park to convert the old Ashbourne to Buxton branch-line railway into a scenic footpath. While this may not be everyone's choice for a pedestrian route, in this case it has provided a walk through beautiful landscape on which you cannot lose your way. Tissington and nearby Hartington are charming backwater hamlets, most famous for their well-dressing ceremonies.

The sister-route of the Tissington Trail, the High Peak Trail, follows another disused railway track, from Cromford to Buxton. The walker who completes the full 17 miles of the Trail will pass through some of the most typical and delightful landscape that Derbyshire has to offer. There are many features of interest, from a Stone Age settlement at Harboro' Rocks, to a relic of the Industrial Revolution at the Middleton Top Engine House near Cromford where the first cotton mill was

built by Thomas Arkwright in 1771. Not far from Cromford are Black Rocks, a rugged gritstone mass popular with climbers as a training ground.

Perhaps most impressive of all is Arbor Low, a Neolithic stone circle situated on Middleton Moor just east of the Trail not far from Newhaven Park. These huge limestone pillars, now flattened, are estimated to be about 4000 years old and are ranked in importance with Stonehenge and Avebury.

In between the limestone crags and moorland sweeps, Derbyshire boasts some very pleasant townships, the most popular of which is Buxton. Buxton is famous for its waters, first appreciated by the Romans, and has retained its reputation as one of the oldest spas in Britain. It is a town of elegant buildings in a setting of natural magnificence. Its claim to be the highest town in England at just over 1000 feet might, with some justification, be disputed by the market town of Alston in Cumbria.

THE PEAK DISTRICT NATIONAL PARK

Bakewell, known as the capital of the Peak District, basks in a sheltered nook of the Wye Valley; the thirteenth-century bridge which spans the Wye is one of the oldest in the country. Bakewell Tarts (more accurately, puddings) made to the original recipe can be bought in the town centre. The local tourist office provides extensive information on the area. One popular spot is Eyam, a small village to the north of Bakewell. There are several places of interest near by, including Sir William's Road, a superb track that rises to almost 1200 feet, giving views over much of the Peak District. Monsal Head, north-west of Bakewell, is another dramatic beauty spot where the river Wye races through a gorge 200 feet below. Bicycles can be hired at Bakewell, and at other centres throughout the Park.

If you still prefer walking-boots to bicycle wheels, you could do worse than to make for Goyt Valley north-west of Buxton. The roads here are closed on Sundays, and a one-way traffic system is in force at other times, which means that the walker can explore in peace and, equally important, in safety. The valley has many fine wooded paths, deep rocky valleys, and a great reservoir which now seems an almost natural part of the landscape.

Rock-climbing is an important sport in the Peak District, and one that is of necessity taken very seriously, as many of these steep outcrops call for skill and experience. They should not be attempted by the novice, however tempting they may appear. One of the most popular climbing locations in the Peaks is Stanage Edge, a magnificent gritstone escarpment some four miles long. It is reached via a steep, winding road called School Lane which starts at the village of Hathersage, about eight miles north of Bakewell. The views from the top are truly superb, towards Manchester in the west and Sheffield in the east. Climbing centres like this one apart, it is possible to find near-solitude and natural silence almost anywhere within the National Park – provided, that is, you are prepared to don walking-boots.

Ordnance Survey maps: 109, 110, 118, 119

Right The Goyt Valley offers pleasant walking in a peaceful setting. The southern part is particularly lovely, where the river is bounded by picturesque moorland slopes.

The North

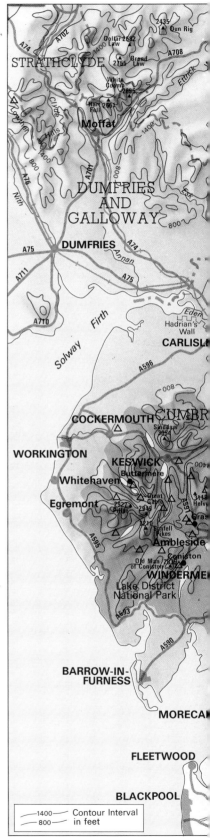

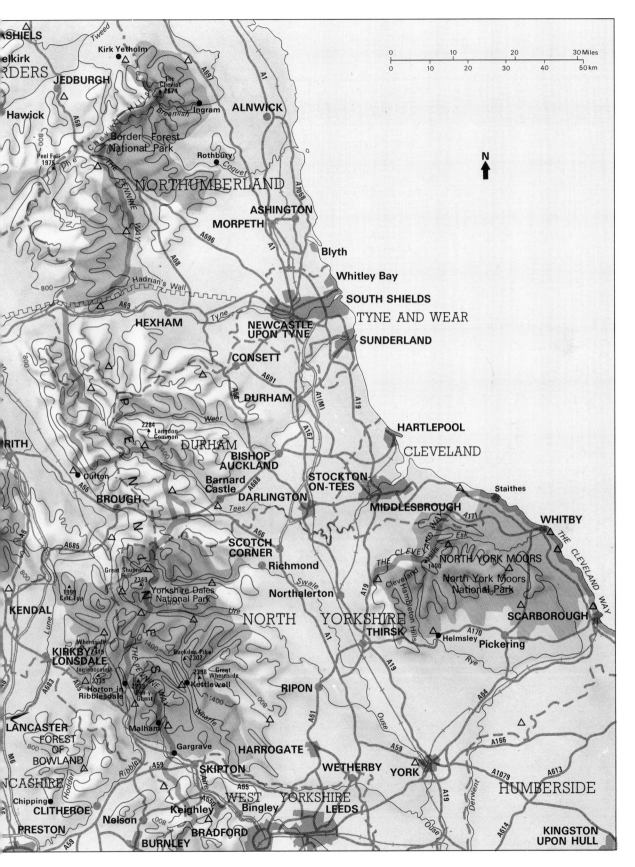

Yorkshire and Lancashire

The Yorkshire Dales National Park

Yorkshire boasts two National Parks, of which the Dales Park is generally considered the gentler. The Dales hold a four-square position astride the central Pennines and are acknowledged as some of the finest hill-walking heights in the whole of Europe.

The moorland tops are wide and wild, in several places rising to 2000 feet and more. They are cross-hatched by contrasting narrow valleys of gritstone or limestone, often rugged at higher levels, but invariably lush-green and beautiful along the lower slopes. These fells form part of the great watershed of England.

The tracks and paths that meander over this area of dry-stone walls and sparkling rivers are nearly all of ancient origin, and many date from prehistoric times. There are so many high spots that it is difficult to know which to advocate first. However, for the first-time visitor with a week or so to spare, there is one stretch which should paint an unforgettable picture: the section of the Pennine Way Path which cuts right through the Dales from north to south. I can personally think of few other stretches of footpath to equal that which winds from Gargrave on the Leeds and Liverpool Canal, up through the Aire Valley via Airton, to Malham and on to the heights of Malham Moor.

Though only a dozen miles or so in length, this section of the Way contains, especially at the northern end, some of the most majestic limestone canyons to be seen anywhere in the country. Created at the dawn of time by major geological contortions (the Mid-Craven Fault), it is a world of quite spectacular cliffs – dazzling white in sunshine – deep-fissured here, pavemented at precipitous heights there, the whole honey-combed by a vast network of caves eroded by water over millions of years.

Malham Cove, where the limestone faces rise to nearly 250 feet, is only fractionally less dramatic than nearby Gordale Scar, a towering canyon 400 feet high with Gordale Beck tumbling from the top in two great spouts. Malham Tarn, a glacial mini-lake formed from an Ice Age moraine, at the summit of the highest limestone scarp in the Pennines (1300 feet), is the final jewel in the chain before the next great open space of Malham Moor. For those with the inclination, and energy, Fountains Fell beckons on the skyline, along a marvellous stretch of old pack-horse trail.

Not much further along the Way, the walker's horizon is suddenly broken again, this time by the majestic summit of Pen-y-Ghent. Though not the highest peak along the route (Cross Fell has that title), it is certainly the most famous, and in some lights really does live up to its local name of the Golden Lion. There is easy footpath access from Horton in Ribblesdale for those approaching the area by road.

The surrounding countryside is a Mecca for pot-holers; Sell Gill Holes, Cross Pot, and Jackdaw Hole are just a few among many. Hawes, the acknowledged half-way house for Pennine Way walkers, is an ancient and mellow market

Right Scabbate Gate near Kettlewell, on the eastern fringe of the National Park.

Below Pen-y-Ghent (2273 feet) from Churn Milk Hole. The view from the summit is one of the finest on the Pennine Way.

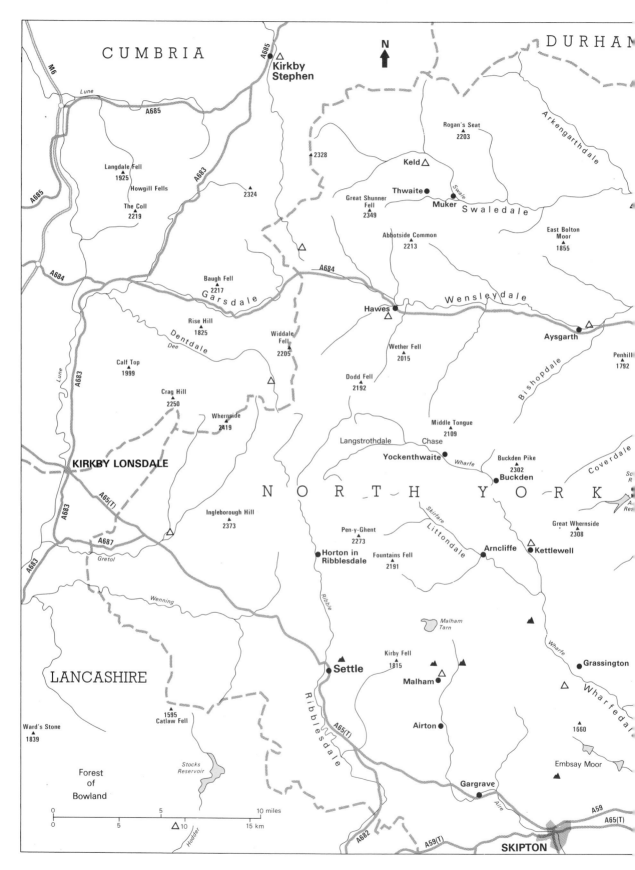

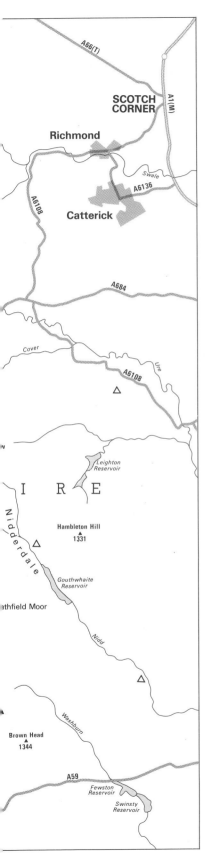

town, a good supply base with a choice of accommodation including a youth hostel and selection of camping-grounds.

Most walkers who pass through Hawes take time to visit the Green Dragon Inn just up the road, where you pass through the pub to see Hardrow Force, which has a clear water drop of 100 feet, making it the highest unbroken cataract in Britain. It is set within a miniature canyon, in formation not unlike those of Arizona. Despite the tamed, and rather commercialized setting, it is worth seeing.

From Wensleydale, the Way passes north to Swaledale, arguably the most beautiful of all the Dales, through a succession of evocatively named hamlets, all visually rich and in heady hill-country settings. A few miles south of Thwaite is Buttertubs Pass, a spectacular ravine amid surrounding hill scallops. There is a youth hostel at Keld, a prettily situated camping-ground at Muker on the banks of the Swale, and the highest, most isolated, pub in England at Tan Hill. Here you are on the roof of a moorland world, 1758 feet above sea level and on the northern fringe of the Dales National Park.

All these riches are contained within what is only a mere strip of the area. On the western side of the river Ribble are two more giant and distinctive summits, Whernside and Ingleborough. These, together with Pen-y-Ghent, form the famous Three Peaks, all of them well over 2000 feet high.

Above View from Hebden Ghyll, overlooking Wharfedale. The area is rich in footpaths providing many fine walks.

The Three Peaks Walk is a challenge that tempts probably every dedicated hill-walker at some time. The shortest distances between the summits are 7¼ miles, 4½ miles, and 8¾ miles, and it really is an accomplishment to complete the circuit in one day. The record is just under 3 hours, set up by Frank Dawson in 1960. The whole of this area provides fine climbing, rock-scrambling, and hill-walking, not to mention pot-holing. Gaping Gill is just one target for subterranean explorers, among the largest outcrops of limestone in Britain, where more than 500 cave systems have been discovered. For me, the area is best epitomized by the ridge walk from just north of Ingleborough to the tarn-studded dome of Whernside; I would strongly recommend you to try it.

On the eastern side of the Park, between Grassington and Aysgarth, the footpaths of Wharfedale provide more fine walking. Three especially enjoyable stretches, offering impressive views, lead respectively from Bolton Abbey to the renowned high point of Simon's Seat at 1592 feet; from Buckden along the old Roman road to Yockenthwaite; and from Kettlewell to Arncliffe. Bolton Abbey village is Yorkshire's best-known beauty spot and Kettlewell already a thriving settlement when the Domesday Book was compiled.

The Forest of Bowland

Between Yockenthwaite and Bainbridge to the north, a Roman road traverses Wether Fell, runs south-west through Ribblehead, and continues into Lancashire. Here, in Ribblesdale, watered by the river Ribble, lies a beautiful, but relatively unknown, stretch of high country: the Forest of Bowland.

Although geographically very close to Blackpool and the resorts of the north-west coast, the Forest of Bowland is still very much the preserve of those who are prepared to seek out the quieter corners of Britain.

It is a landscape that has hardly changed since the Industrial Revolution, 300 square miles of moorland dotted with secluded wooded dales. You can walk almost all day without meeting another person, even in high summer. The geology is similar to that of the Pennine range on the other side of the Ribble Valley.

The central region has only a few scattered villages and there are no major roads. It is one of the few remaining havens of natural peace, all the more astounding given its position a few miles east of the busy M6 motorway.

Clitheroe, which forms the peak of a three-town triangle with Blackburn and Burnley, is one of the most strategic bases for exploring the area. It is a charming, friendly, and unpretentious little town, dominated by mighty Pendle Hill, a looming whale-back 1830 feet above sea level. The town has existed since Saxon times and is still graced by a bold Norman castle. There is a well-run municipal touring park on the banks of the Ribble, not far from the town centre.

If you want to see the countryside by car, one fine route would be to take the B6478 north-west across Bradford Fell. The approach is one of breath-taking delight, peak after peak rising skywards, then a final swoop down to the pretty hamlet of Newton. The village, blending with the limestone hill of Dunnow Rock, is watered by the river Hodder, winding its slow course from the bridge to join the Ribble.

For more fine panoramas, this time actively earned, take one of the footpaths to the summit of Pendle Hill. The views from the 7-mile-long plateau are as impressive as any in the kingdom. The ascent is relatively easy, the reward in good weather infinitely worthwhile.

There is a choice of minor roads from Clitheroe, but if you can, go via Downham just to the north-east which is claimed to be the prettiest village in Lancashire. At the heart of the area is the Trough of Bowland, a regal canyon between high fells. For my part, if this were the only area of beauty in Lancashire, it alone would make the journey worthwhile. There are a number of areas of special access, negotiated between the local authorities and landowners, covering something like 3000 acres of remote Bowland, which are now available to leisure walkers.

Clough Pike rewards the wanderer with glorious scenes, with panoramic views as far as the Lake District. Fairsnape Fell and Wolf Fell (reached from the village of Chipping just south of the Trough) are equally impressive and have a well-marked network of footpaths. The going is hard in places, and also splendidly rough and remote. It is not really countryside for the novice walking alone, and excursions of any length should not be undertaken lightly. The access areas are patrolled by special rangers who will help anyone in difficulty. For the walker with the right gear and basic knowledge, though, Bowland must be short-listed as one of the least-tramped and therefore – in some ways – the best fell-walking districts in Britain.

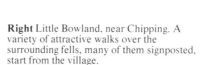
Right Little Bowland, near Chipping. A variety of attractive walks over the surrounding fells, many of them signposted, start from the village.

The North York Moors National Park

Back across the Pennines to the east lie the North Yorkshire Moors, mostly contained within the county's second National Park. It is a landscape of regal proportions, of lofty moorland and wide horizons, divided and softened – often in the most striking way – by defile valleys and ancient settlements as mellow as they are picturesque.

Hutton-le-Hole on the south flank of the high moors is proudly proclaimed the prettiest village in all Yorkshire. Contrasting strongly, almost savagely when the wind is keening, is the tiny and aptly named Cold Kirby. And just a stone's throw from this wind-swept, almost desolate, setting there is Sutton Bank, offering a truly breath-taking viewpoint.

North Yorkshire is a county of contrasts, therefore, the western half dominated by the Cleveland and Hambleton Hills, the eastern swathe highlighted by a coastline as rugged as the hinterland in parts yet distinctly different in character. This stern but beautiful countryside is an established favourite of the long-distance walker and is blessed with some fine pedestrian routes. There is the horseshoe Cleveland Way which winds for a hundred miles almost right round the National Park boundary, from Helmsley to Filey; the oddly named Lyke Wake Walk, a 40-mile traverse of the wild central plateau

from Osmotherley to Ravenscar; and countless shorter high-country routes in between.

By way of introduction to this huge and handsome area, here are just a few personal favourites to whet the appetite. As a start, and one with a number of built-in delights, the first dozen miles or so of the Cleveland Way could hardly be bettered. It begins at Helmsley, a market town whose Norman origins are proclaimed by the barbican and gatehouse of the ruined fortress. Most walkers make a detour to see the imposing ruins of Rievaulx Abbey, founded by the Cistercian order in 1131, which lie just north of the Way outside the town. From the Abbey a magnificent woodland path ascends at once above the river Wye – just one of five rivers that flow through the North Yorks Moors from north to south – and winds among limestone clefts and outcrops. Splendid views open sporadically between forestry plantations as you pass Cold Kirby where the lush valleys are left behind.

If the wind pipes up and the clouds scud, the walker will experience the true raw edge of the northern climate, but it is undeniably invigorating, with Sutton Bank a most worthy objective. From this sheer scarp, the result of an immense geological upheaval, breath-taking vistas open up across Gormire Lake and the road to Thirsk far below. Hood Hill stands out from the surrounding lowland,

with half Yorkshire, seemingly, stretching away beyond.

A little further along the Hambleton ridge (where there is a comprehensive information centre and a café) there is a short detour path to Roulston Scar which offers further magnificent views.

There is a youth hostel at Helmsley and another at Osmotherley which also has ample alternative accommodation, but it is some 22 miles between the two. The second section, 14 hard miles from Sutton Bank along the western rim of the Hambleton Hills, is precipitous in parts and rightly the province of the experienced fell-walker; the novice should not attempt it alone.

At Osmotherley there are some fine local stretches to explore in addition to the Cleveland Way. This is also the starting-point of the Lyke Wake Walk, whose name derives from an ancient dirge about a wandering ghost; a coffin badge is awarded to those who complete the rugged 40-mile moorland crossing within twenty-four hours. Thousands succeed every year, so it is not all that forbidding (the track is by now clearly defined for the whole distance), but again it is wide and wild, with little in between and definitely not terrain to be tackled on a whim.

Some thousand feet above the village of Osmotherley, the Cleveland Way and the Lyke Wake Walk coincide for 12 miles, and this stretch is sometimes quite

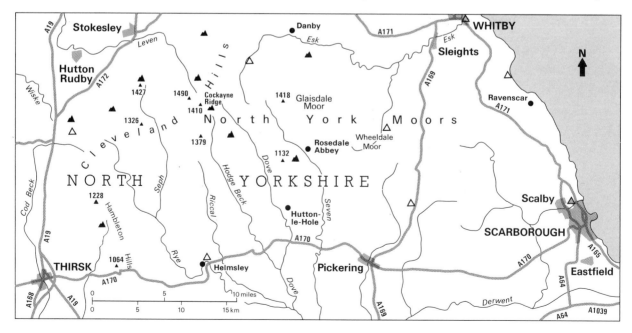

crowded during summer week-ends. For softer, greener contours, though only slightly less dramatic, take the un-classified minor road from the village to Hawnby along a route which undulates between voluptuous folds of the hills and offers a number of intriguing footpaths to explore. The country is given over to sheep and heather, with the grey-stone hamlet of Hawnby tucked away above the river Rye.

For yet more lofty delights, leave the trans-Yorkshire A170 at Pickering and penetrate northwards to Rosedale Abbey. Now you are well on the way to the highest point of the National Park which tops the 1400-foot mark over Glaisdale Moor just to the north of Rosedale. There is a camping-ground owned by the Forestry Commission just north of Cropton village, and another along the same minor road close to Rosedale Abbey which gives access to some spectacular walking amid high and lonely country.

There is a stretch of surprisingly well-preserved Roman road between Goat-land village (itself a renowned beauty spot, famous for its huge village green and the nearby waterfalls) and Wheel-

Above Farndale Moor from Gillamoor. From Hutton-le-Hole, at the entrance to the moor, a panoramic route leads across the valley heads.

dale Moor. This probably ran from Whitby to York, though only a couple of miles still remain. A wealth of information about North Yorkshire is available from Danby Lodge National Park Centre, located north of Danby High Moor in the Esk Valley. Walk from the Centre to explore Little Fryup Dale and Great Fryup Dale, or wander through Danby Dale, rich in ancient cairns and burial mounds.

For grandeur of a different kind, take the road north-east from Danby to Staithes on the coast. Staithes has remained an enclave of old Yorkshire, a hard-working, tight-knit seafaring community where the old methods of fishery are still practised. The Cleveland Way passes through Staithes on its route north, hugging the coast and revealing fine views at every point. For one of the finest, walk to Skinningrove, just north of Staithes, where the cliff-path brings you to the pinnacle of Boulby Cliff, at 660 feet the highest sea cliffs in England, a dizzyingly exhilarating experience.

Whitby, 12 miles north of Staithes, a near-perfect deep-water harbour sheltered from all but the northerly wind, is a visual delight with its straggle of colourful houses clinging to each bank of the river Esk which slices through the town. Cook's ships *Endeavour* and *Resolution* were built in the yards here. The Way takes in the 999 steps which pass the seamen's church and lead to the ruins of the thirteenth-century Abbey. The same rugged beauty of this coastline awaits the walker all the way to Ravenscar and beyond, offering a heady diet of outstanding scenic delight.

Ordnance Survey maps: 93, 94, 98–104

Right View from Sutton Bank over Gormire Lake in its woodland setting, with the Dales and the Lake District in the distance.

Cumbria

Competing with Devonshire as the most visited of all the English counties, Cumbria contains the highest, fiercest volcanic peaks in the land. Here is the home of England's highest mountain, just one of a hundred or more topping the 2000-foot mark, double that number if all lesser peaks are included. It is, quite simply, Britain's finest natural playground. Between the groups of massive humped fells and volcanic crags, the result of violent activity 450 million years ago, are those other jewels, the eight major lakes which were formed when the Ice Age glaciers melted and which give the Lake District its name.

Despite the seasonally inclement weather, the mass influx of visitors in the summer months, the crowded roads and lack of accommodation, the allure of the Lake District remains irresistible. Yet in the high season, only those visitors who are prepared to don walking-boots will be rewarded by moments of the real magic that Lakeland can bestow. Others who seek the often elusive tranquillity of this mountain fastness must choose the spring or autumn, each beautiful in its separate way. In winter, the Lake District is strictly the province of climbing tigers and the very hardiest of hill-walkers.

Eastern Cumbria

Yet Cumbria is not just the Lake District. The eastern sector of the county, beyond the wide Eden Valley, is blessed with an enchanted empty quarter made up of much princely, if not regal, terrain. Here, where Cumbria flirts with neighbouring county Durham, there is much to satisfy the lover of high country.

Again this little bit of secret England is only revealed in all its splendour to those ready to tramp a few miles of the Pennine Way. After leaving North Yorkshire, the Way strikes east to cross a corner of Durham along a stretch of the river Tees, before veering westwards across a corner of Cumbria. It fetches up briefly at Dufton before turning north again, and it is here you find splendour comparable, in its way, with that further west. What is certain is that you will be

Below Mardale Beck, near Haweswater in the eastern region of Lakeland.

Right Eskdale, south-western Lakeland. This is a splendid base for the Scafell and Bowfell mountain ranges.

Above The source of the river Tyne rising in the mountains to the east of Cross Fell, the highest point in the Pennines.

Opposite High Cup Nick (1900 feet) offers one of the finest viewpoints in some of the most rugged countryside along the Pennine Way. View south-west down High Cup Gill.

able to savour it in near-solitude, even in the height of summer.

First to Dufton itself, disdainfully and delightfully unimpressed with progress, one of those intriguing villages that somehow instils instant and permanent affection. A settlement since Saxon times, it has a splendid wide main street and buildings of warm sandstone. There are a couple of camping-grounds close by, well placed for access to two high-country gems, High Cup Nick and Cross Fell. The first, reached by a wide and ancient hill-track south-east from Dufton, is an awesome scenic surprise, even for the most blasé. From the razor-edge rim of this vast scalloped chasm, a massive half-moon of dolerite cliffs buttressed with jagged tops plummets almost sheer for a thousand feet. Far below, the floor of this moonscape glacial amphitheatre is scattered with rocks broken from Whin Sill. If there is one location that epitomizes the stark majesty characteristic of the Pennine Way, this surely must be it.

From this superb vantage point, distant horizons reveal the western side of the county, with Skiddaw and Coniston Old Man dominating the far skyline. Dufton Pike rises like a giant burial mound in the middle distance, with the green and contrastingly tranquil Vale of Eden falling away southwards. On a bright day when visibility is good, it will be a moment to recall years later.

Even higher country lies just to the north-east of Dufton, harder country too, both to ascend and to traverse, across one of the loneliest stretches of the Pennine Way. It is another magnetic draw though, if the weather is kindly, with Cross Fell, the highest of the Pennine Way summits, as the reward.

Although not as pronounced, nor as shapely, as any of the famous Three Peaks, the brooding Cross Fell is none the less king at 2930 feet. The route is arduous in places, crossing Knock Fell, Great Dun Fell, and Skirwith Fell, but the views from this immense sky-scraping plateau stretch as far as the Scottish border. If you have ever longed for the liberating, exhilarating feeling of being on the roof of the world, then this is where you will find it.

The Lake District National Park

Anyone who has negotiated Striding Edge to the summit of Helvellyn, or has seen the sun rise from that most beautiful of all England's mountains, Great Gable, will know that the Lake District proffers the ultimate of heady wines to the hill-walker. The problem for the majority of first-time visitors, however, is how to reach these magnificent and celebrated heights. Preparation is the answer, with study of large-scale maps, frequent reference to the seven invaluable guide-books by Wainwright, and a careful selection of the relevant areas.

Although the Lake District is the largest of England's National Parks and encompasses 866 square miles, its geography is crowded and complex, and getting from one section to another by road is seldom straightforward. On a first visit it is probably best to explore one area in depth, rather than attempt to take in the whole of the Park. Whichever area you select, it is bound to be memorable.

The Park is divided into two unofficial areas – with lake Windermere the focal point in the south, and Keswick at the centre of the northern district – and it is along this rough dividing line that the real high country is situated, dominated by Shap Fell, Helvellyn, and Scafell Pike, the highest English peak, which rises to 3210 feet.

The southern area, around Windermere, Grasmere, and Coniston, is the most well known and hence the most crowded. There is pleasant and easy walking around all the major lakes, and the routes are well marked. For a real sense of exhilaration, however, the serious walker will turn to the high ground, to the 'roots of Heaven' as it is known in local legend. And it is almost invariably the highest peaks that exert the biggest draw: Scafell, Scafell Pike, and Great Gable.

The route you must take to reach a strategic base from which to tackle this trio of giant peaks is itself dramatic, west from Ambleside on a minor road that winds up over Wrynose and Hard Knott Passes. Hard Knott Pass is nearly 1300 feet high and one of the toughest but most exciting motoring challenges in the Lake District.

The Romans built a fort on the summit of Hard Knott in the second century, one of several stations on the route from Ravenglass to Penrith; the ruins of the fort can still be seen. From the top of the Pass the road runs steeply down to

Eskdale, then doubles back via Santon Bridge to end at Wasdale Head, where there is a youth hostel, a camping-ground, and a hotel.

A whole variety of hill-tracks and mountain paths is literally on the doorstep, the best the Lake District holds, but although most of the recognized paths are clearly defined and the going is not too strenuous (at least on the lower slopes), the inexperienced walker should not venture on to the tops alone or in poor weather conditions.

One summit among many you might consider if conditions are favourable is Great Gable (2949 feet). There are numerous routes to the summit, the most direct from the signposted path at the summit of Sty Head Pass. The approach can be made from either Wasdale or Borrowdale. For a longer, equally dramatic route, there is a signposted path marked by cairns leading from the top of Honister Pass via Green Gable. This single walk should make you a confirmed lover of the Lake District if

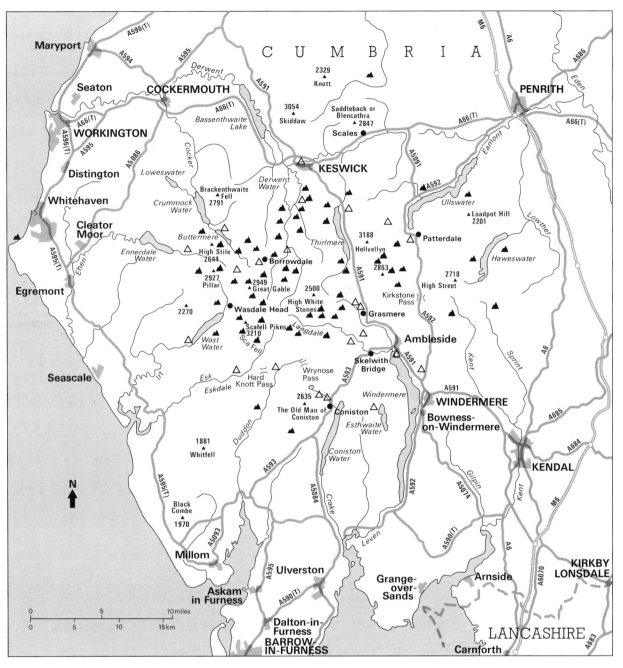

you are not one already. There are many redoubtable climbing faces on Great Gable, of which Napes Needle is one, an elegant and enticing rock pillar tempting all those addicted to the vertical game. As a rule, the Scafell range and the area between Pillar and Great Gable is less crowded than the high country above Borrowdale or Langdale. Certainly these Western fells are the most rugged.

Another firm favourite – and extremely popular with hill-walkers of all grades – is the Helvellyn summit via Striding

Edge. The walk along this razor-edge path is one of the most spectacular in Lakeland and is only dangerous in the most severe winter conditions. The best approach is from a parking area alongside the A591 in Patterdale, midway between Keswick and Grasmere. There are numerous alternative routes to the summit, but this 3-mile ascent and traverse is the classic one.

Keswick, an ancient market town now bustling with tourists, is a good centre from which to explore Borrowdale, one

Opposite Hard Knott Pass rises to almost 1300 feet at the approach to Eskdale en route to the most majestic of the Lakeland peaks.

Above The long sweep of Wastwater, bounded by Great Gable (centre) and Scafell Pike, England's highest mountain (right). Wasdale is the best centre in the district for rock-climbing.

Opposite The Langdale Pikes west of Grasmere are one of the favourite groups of mountains in the Lake District. They are easily accessible and the circuit can be completed within a day of fairly easy walking.

of Lakeland's most scenic valleys, and the surrounding mountain ranges. Just north-west of Keswick mighty Skiddaw rises to over 3000 feet, and to the north-east Blencathra (known also as Saddleback), equally impressive. There is a superb path to the top of Blencathra from Scales, starting behind the White Horse Inn. The panorama from the top of Blencathra is one of the most extensive, and most unobscured, in Lakeland.

Second only in popularity to the Scafell group of mountains are the Langdale Pikes, which are best reached via the B5343 from Skelwith Bridge west of Ambleside. The New Dungeon Ghyll Hotel at the top end of the dale is a great gathering point of walkers and climbers. There is a camping-ground near by which, despite its size, is often full in the summer.

The Langdale Pikes have two principal summits, Pike o' Stickle (2323 feet) and Harrison Stickle (2401 feet), the latter being predominant. Again there

are several routes, but the most popular begins at the hotel. The ascent begins with a stiffish haul to Stickle Tarn. From here there are paths to Pavey Ark ridge and, for bolder adventurers, the track across the prominent ledge known as Jacks Rake. On this one you come about as close to free climbing as is prudent. These are just two among a whole variety of short and medium-distance hill-walks in the vicinity.

In conclusion, a few practical points for those who want to camp. Owing to the popularity of the Lake District, during the high season it is becoming almost obligatory to book a pitch in advance whenever possible. As the sites inside the Park are often over-stretched, or do not always accept bookings, one solution is to make your base outside the Park.

On the southern fringes, the Grange-over-Sands area may prove fruitful, as there are several large holiday and touring parks hereabouts, or in the north, the coastal strip below Silloth. It does mean

that you can only make day trips to the hills, of course, but by way of recompense you will almost certainly enjoy more hours of good weather.

If proximity is imperative, on the other hand, there are a number of large touring parks where you might be able to find a pitch, even at the height of the season. The large camping-park just north of Windermere on the A592, located at the foot of Kirkstone Pass, is one possibility, and there are two spacious grounds close to Coniston, off the A593. A comprehensive list of touring grounds is contained in the booklet 'Sites for Caravans and Tents', which is published by the National Park Information Service.

The Cumbria Tourist Board provides a very efficient information service to accompany its programme of organized pursuits. For mountain-lovers particularly, there are tuition and expedition centres based at Wasdale Head, Langdale, Coniston, Buttermere, and Borrowdale, which are organized by Outward Bound schools and the Lake District Planning Board. There are also professional guides based at Patterdale, Keswick, and a number of other centres. There are 20 youth hostels within the Park boundaries based on all the recognized hill-walking and climbing areas.

Ordnance Survey maps: 89, 90, 91, 96, 97, 98

Right Castle Cräg near Grange. Borrowdale is an ideal walking centre and offers access to some of the most spectacular scenery in Lakeland.

Opposite above The smooth ridge of Blencathra, also known as Saddleback, rises to 2847 feet north of the village of Threlkeld, north-east of Keswick.

Opposite below Skiddaw (3054 feet) from the river Derwent at Portinscale, Keswick.

Northumberland

Above The North Tyne. Much of Northumberland is covered with wide sweeps of forest, the most extensive tract in Britain.

Opposite Whitfield Moor, near Haltwhistle. The town is a convenient base from which to explore Hadrian's Wall.

Northumberland has been dubbed 'The Forgotten County', but this would seem to be something of a misnomer, with Allendale in its lofty moorland setting claiming to be the geographical centre of Britain, and Hadrian's Wall stretching across the county for 73 miles as a reminder of the area's strategic importance as the frontier of England's northern boundary from Roman times. Certainly, on a summer day, dodging excursion coaches around Housesteads Fort, or looking vainly for a parking spot in Hexham, it could be seen as some sour joke. But step aside just a little from such bustling centres to discover the accuracy of this local tag for yourself; and a delightful truth it is in the learning.

For Northumberland is also 'The Big Country', with massive sweeps of landscape which in places is wide and wild enough to vie with the finest in Yorkshire. Much of it is covered with trees, part of the Border Forest National Park, the biggest in the British Isles, rivalling Germany's Black Forest in extent.

North of Bellingham, the narrowing North Tyne Valley becomes the only route through the Forest, and only isolated hill farms are to be seen at intervals along the twenty-odd miles to

the Scottish border. Between the great tree plantations – mainly Norway and Sitka Spruce – stand open hill ranges with special appeal for those who like the challenge of distance-walking. This is not cosy country, though, with a pub or hamlet just over the next brow, more likely a half day's tramp or longer over a succession of hills before some isolated haven comes into view.

This could be called adventure terrain, and is not really the domain of the stroller. For those with stout boots and a spirit to match, the acknowledged base is the Forestry Commission camping-ground at Lewisburn, some fifteen miles north-west of Bellingham, which is itself well off the tourist route straddling the B6320 north of Hexham. The only other permanent settlement in this splendid hill wilderness is a forestry village, Kielder. A wide selection of tracks have been laid out through the Forest; they meander for miles, linking the surrounding dales and running on into Scotland.

One possibility is to take the path north from the camping-ground, cross over into Redesdale via Kielderhead Moor and Oh Me Edge (elevation 1800 feet), and from there into Scotland over the Roman road past Chew Green Fort

on a great spur of the Cheviots. Peel Fell, the highest point of the Border Forest Park at 1975 feet, can be seen en route approximately seven miles from the camping-ground. From this border summit there are views from the North Sea to the Solway Firth.

Another fine walk follows the old Border Raider's route, past Kielder Stone to Carter Fell, then on to Bonchester Bridge on Scottish territory. To the south there is yet more majestic fell-walking, this time over a choice of tracks that fetch up in the vicinity of Christianbury Crag (1600 feet) on the border of Cumbria. If you really want high country to yourself for an active, yet recuperative, spell, this is one part of Britain where you will find it, in the middle of August or any other time.

The same cannot be said, unfortunately, for Hadrian's Wall, the most perfectly preserved and dramatic relic of Roman rule outside Italy. Yet it is possible to avoid some of the crowds: the camper or caravanner could make a base at the racecourse site 1½ miles from the centre of Hexham or at the touring site just off the A69 east of Haltwhistle. Both these towns are conveniently placed for exploration of the Wall and the principal Roman remains in the area. Hexham, a historic yet lively market town with many fine twelfth- and fourteenth-century buildings, is set in a beautiful location on the banks of the Tyne. Much of the stone used to build the older parts of the town was pillaged from the Wall.

The choice of Roman remains is wide and varied, from Corbridge and Chesters in the east, to Housesteads, Steel Rigg, and Walltown Crags in the west. At Vindolanda, 5 miles from Haltwhistle, there is a fine frontier fort and settlement where many exciting archaeological discoveries have recently been made and work is still in progress.

For a particularly spectacular section of the Wall, take the B6318 eastwards from Greenhead that follows the sharply etched line of Winshields Crag. The turn-off to Cawfields leads to a car park and the start of an unforgettable 8-mile walk along the Wall itself to Crag Lough, or further if you will, to Chesters and the town of Wall in the North Tyne Valley.

Housesteads Fort (Vercovicium) is the most famous, and most visited, place along the Wall. It is certainly worth a visit, despite the crowds, for in addition to the superbly preserved remains there is a fascinating museum. Whichever of the Roman sites you explore, try to do so early in the day to capture an echo of that earlier civilization. One wonders how the garrison cohorts, particularly those from the Mediterranean, endured this far-northern posting, as the climate was

Above View from the lower slopes of the Cheviot towards Harthope Burn.

probably not significantly different from what it is today. Trekking the Whin Sill crags is distinctly invigorating even in high summer, while in winter it can be a real test of endurance.

The major change since the time of the Roman settlement in the second century is to be found in the landscape to the north of the Wall. What was once open, high moorland is now the vast Wark Forest, with scenery more reminiscent of Canada than England. Although there is much divided opinion among conservationists about large-scale afforestation, in the case of the Northumbrian forests the Forestry Commission provides first-class camping-grounds and countless footpaths, which have made the area accessible to all.

The minor B6320 road north from the little town of Wall through the village of Wark and on to Bellingham is a delightful route through green forest scattered with high, open fells and isolated hill farms, with wide skies and wider horizons; and (with luck) scarcely another car to be seen.

Wark, a charming and ancient village on the North Tyne river, is a good base for a variety of walking expeditions.

Above A dramatic stretch of path leads along the Roman wall to Crag Lough.

Left From Peel Fell (1975 feet), the highest point of the Border Forest Park, there are fine views from the North Sea to the Solway Firth.

There is inn accommodation and a camping-ground set on the river bank to the north-east of the village. One attractive route follows Wark Burn which wends west from the North Tyne and meets up with the lengthy Pennine Way between Wark and Stonehaugh, 5 miles away, where there is another camping-ground, administered by the Forestry Commission.

For those who want to tackle the stiffer walking of the Pennine Way, Bellingham provides an excellent base. It is a bustling, friendly market town with good facilities, a youth hostel, and information centre. Although now rather given over to tourism, the town still remains a meeting-place for hill farmers and a famous cattle market is held there. One popular local walk leads from the town up the steep-sided valley of Hareshaw Burn to Hareshaw Linn, one of the prettiest waterfalls in the county.

It takes time, and repeated visits, to discover the natural attractions of the National Park. The Simonside hill range to the south of Rothbury is just one of many. Hill-tracks run for 10 miles and more along the top of these sandstone heights with their characteristic stepped contours, to the summit of Tosson Hill, 1447 feet above sea level. From this lofty viewpoint you can follow the route of the river Coquet to the North Sea, while to the west the rolling Cheviots form a natural frontier wall with Scotland.

To the south-west beyond Coquetdale lies Redesdale, once a turbulent frontier region where the Battle of Otterburn (better known as Chevy Chase) was fought in 1388. There is scenic walking along the banks of the river Rede. North-west of Otterburn is Rochester where the Pennine Way once more dominates the scene. The long-distance path follows the river Rede here, then veers north below Byrness on the A68.

This is a superb stretch of rugged country for the walker, running parallel at first with Dere Street (once the Roman route from York to the North), passing a Roman camp just on the English side of the border. There is an army firing range near by, but due warning is always given. The Path then continues to Beef Stand Hill (1845 feet), aptly named as herds of Highland cattle and Galloways graze these majestic wind-swept heights. Here the Path crosses for the first time into Scotland.

Beyond Windy Gyle, approached via a prairie-like sweep of grassland, and reaching 2034 feet at the summit, a path branches off from the main Way back into Northumberland to the Cheviot summit plateau, 2675 feet high. The Cheviot range is Devonian in origin, formed by volcanic upheaval and softened during the glacial periods, resulting in voluptuous rounded contours. Underfoot, it is a terrain of tussock grasses, peat hags, and clumps of heather. Between the steep-sided clefts and valleys which fall away on either side of

the Path are revealed the pinkish granite outcrops and scree slopes. It is a remote area, not for the casual stroller.

It is nearly thirty miles between Bellingham and Kirk Yetholm, the northern terminal of the Pennine Way, if you include the ascent of the Cheviot summit; hard miles at that, with not a great deal between save the tiny hamlet of Byrness, where there is a youth hostel and a camping-ground. A comfort to newcomers is the full-time Warden Service, which operates over the whole of the National Park at week-ends and during school holidays. This voluntary service aims to advise and help visitors to enjoy the countryside.

A less arduous and much shorter route to the summit of the Cheviot is via Wooler to the north-east. A track from Langleeford alongside the Harthope Burn, just south-west of the town, is the acknowledged starting-point for the 3-mile ascent. Wooler is a good base from which to explore a number of fine tracks

over the Cheviots; one hill walk among many which is certain to please is over Humbleton Hill to the 1180-foot summit of Yeavering Bell where there is a huge Iron Age fort. From the site of the fort there are sweeping vistas across the Milfield Plain towards Bamburgh Castle and Lindisfarne on the coast. There is a pleasant touring park situated on the river Breamish not far from Wooler off the A697 near Powburn village.

The stretch of coast between Bamburgh and Lindisfarne is popular with tourists in the summer, and for lovers of high and lonely places the Northumbrian hinterland is the real magnet. Information on hill-walking in the National Park is available from the centres at Ingram in the Cheviots; Rothbury in Coquetdale; Byrness in Upper Redesdale; and Once Brewed, west of Bardon Mill (Hadrian's Wall).

Ordnance Survey maps: 74, 75, 80, 81, 86, 87, 88

Above left The Cheviot range from Langleeford, south-west of Wooler.

Above Harehaugh British Camp near Rothbury in the eastern part of the National Park. Well-marked hill-tracks criss-cross the area.

Scotland

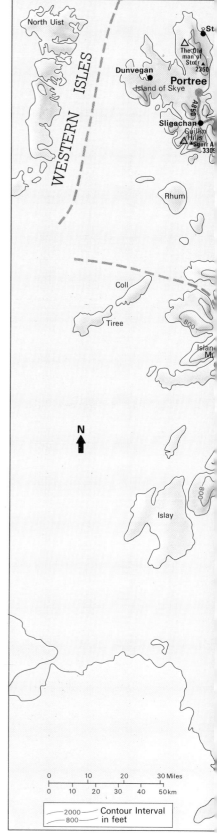

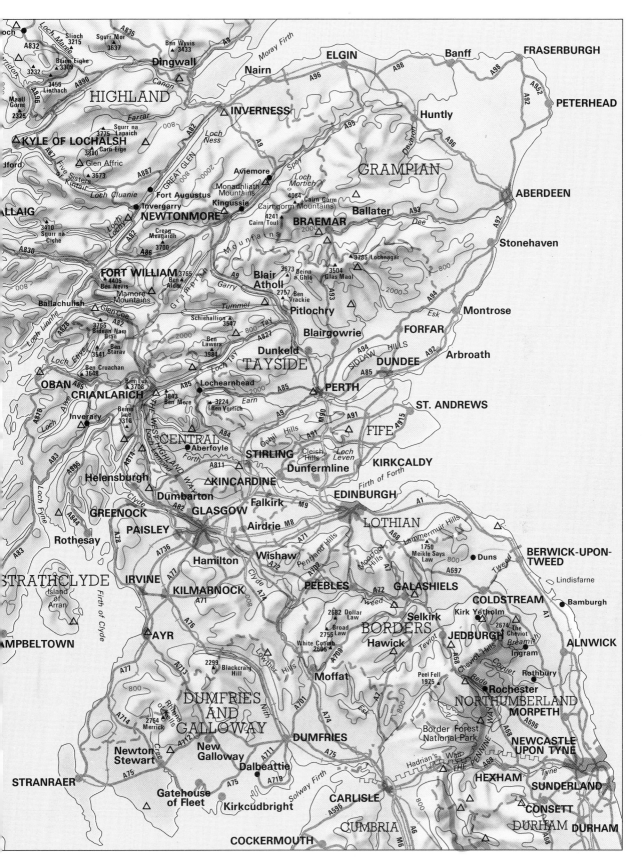

Southern Scotland

Berkwickshire

The border region around Berwick-on-Tweed which straddles both Scotland and England was historically often disputed between the two countries, and even today this ambiguity lingers on. Berwick, on the north side of the river Tweed, is geographically in Scotland, but is included for administrative purposes in the county of Northumberland. For all that, the town still serves as the Anglo-Scottish border and is an ideal starting-point for an exploration of southern Scotland.

The A1 is the main route north, but to enjoy a beautiful backwater of Scotland virtually at once, take the branch road to Eyemouth and on to Coldingham and St Abb's. A short walk from the village brings you to St Abb's Head, the most spectacular promontory on this stretch of coast, rising to more than 300 feet. The gin-clear water makes the area popular with skin-divers. There is a well-run camping-ground situated near the beach and harbour.

To the north-west, on the borders of Berwickshire and Lothian, lie the Lammermuir Hills, which offer a wealth of inviting high spots. A convenient base from which to explore this hill strip will be found at Duns, a pleasant town which also has a municipal camping-ground.

Three miles north of Duns is Harden's Hill and a track that winds for some fourteen miles (with one or two short road stretches) over the Lammermuirs to Cockburnspath on the coast, crossing the impressive Whiteadder water on its way. A little west of here is Long-formacus and the equally picturesque Watch Water reservoir. This is a popular walking area as well-marked tracks run from the car park north to the White-adder reservoir and south, around Twin-law Cairns (1466 feet), down to the fringes of Lauderdale. Like Northumberland, this heather-covered high country is sparsely settled and the distances between settlements are often surprisingly long. Those walkers who seek solitude will love it.

Peebles is centrally placed as a starting-point for two more superb high-level routes, across the Moorfoot Hills to the north and Ettrick Forest southwards. An interesting hill-path winds from Peebles hydro along well-defined tracks and forestry roads for some dozen miles, rising gently but progressively to 1736 feet, before descending almost as gently to Craighope on Leithen Water. It is a 6-mile stroll from here, down valley, to Innerleithen. A mile west of Peebles is Neidpath Castle, once a fortress of the Border Fraser clan, besieged but never taken by Cromwell in 1650. To the south is Cademuir Hill; there is a large Iron Age settlement, including two forts, set up on the ridge. Some intriguing sturdy boulder defences still remain.

The minor B709 road is a scenic link-route between Innerleithen on the A72 and St Mary's Loch south alongside the A708. From this spot there is another minor road running west along Megget Water, then a hill-track to Broad Law, the second highest hill in southern Scotland, at 2756 feet. The path is easy and cannot be missed as it follows a fence to the summit where there is a radio beacon. A wide grassy plateau links this hill with Dollar Law (2682 feet) 4 miles away, memorable for its remote setting.

Lofty they may be, but none of the hills in the southern Scottish uplands exceeds 2800 feet, while there are few of the corries or ridge buttresses so typical of the Highland ranges. They do enjoy rather better weather though on the whole. Arguably the finest group of border hills are those between Moffat Water and the headwaters of the river Tweed.

Most holiday drivers going north on the main motorway route leave Moffat behind, thinking that the splendid high country all about them (especially over Beattock Summit) is just the beginning.

So it is in a way if the Highlands are the final objective, but there is much low country in between, and it is worth stopping off in order not to miss some of south Scotland's finest hill country. ·

Moffat, now a quiet and delightful backwater since the advent of the motor road, is a strategic base from which to explore. Just under 10 miles from Moffat is the Grey Mare's Tail, a magnificent waterfall, one of the highest in Scotland, cascading some 200 feet down the escarpment. It is now protected by the National Trust for Scotland.

Footpaths ascend either side of the Tail Burn, steep sided, narrow, and slippery when wet. The track which traverses the north-east side of the gorge is the longest and best, since it continues to Loch Skeen, 2 miles from any road. From there, a route leads to the summit of White Coomb (2695 feet), the highest hill in this group.

Hart Fell (2651 feet) is another popular excursion from Moffat. It can be reached from the Devil's Beef Tub on the Dumfries county line, or from Capplegill on the A708. This is a scenically delightful route, across Swatte Fell and on via a high ridge path to Hart Fell. For those with energy to spare, there are also long-distance paths converging on Moffat. From Tushielaw north-east via Ettrick Water (20 miles); and from Tweedsmuir due north via Fruid reservoir and Glencraigie Burn (16 miles).

Opposite Grey Mare's Tail waterfall, near Moffat. There are two magnificent marked walks to the cliff-top above the falls, giving spectacular views over Moffat Water.

Below The heather-clad slopes of the Lammermuir Hills to the south-east of Edinburgh offer fine walking to lovers of solitude.

Galloway

Those travellers who have ever turned left above Carlisle and taken the Solway route to western Galloway will surely agree that the term 'Lowland' is not strictly accurate. In this far corner of southern Scotland it is descriptive of latitude rather than elevation. Indeed, around Loch Trool there is a cluster of granite peaks distinctly reminiscent of Highland terrain; not surprising, since geologically they are one and the same.

The one large town en route is Dumfries, famous for its association with Burns and Robert the Bruce. For all nature-lovers, especially those visiting early or late in the season, Caerlaverock Wildfowl Trust is an irresistible magnet a few miles south of Dumfries. One of the great wildlife reserves of the north is to be found here, where the river Nith spills into the Solway Firth. There are over a thousand acres of wild shoreline, seasonally a refuge for thousands of Barnacle Geese. There are many observation hides and visitors are welcome between 1 September and 15 May.

From Dumfries the direct road to Dalbeattie is the A711, but the A710 coast road is the more interesting. Mabie Forest is one of the attractions, Sweetheart Abbey another, and the high-level views over the Solway on the approach to Rockcliffe and Kippford can be very impressive in the right light. There are marvellous views from these picturesque small-boat havens across the Solway to Hestan Island. There are touring parks at Kippford, Dalbeattie, and in the nearby market town of Castle Douglas in a loch-side setting.

A few miles out of Dumfries on the A710 lies the village of New Abbey, with Loch Kindar to the south. A lane leading from the Loch forms the beginning of the ascent of Criffel (1866 feet); it is a comparatively easy climb and the views from the summit are splendid, stretching as far as the Lakeland mountains, the Isle of Man, and the Cheviots.

Another magnificent stretch of rugged coast awaits those taking the A75, particularly in the vicinity of Gatehouse of Fleet where there is a large camping-ground. The real beauty of Galloway awaits beyond Newton Stewart in the Galloway National Forest Park and Loch Trool, reached via the A714. There is a Forestry Commission camping-park in a beautiful setting in the

Below The wooded, gently undulating landscape near Dalbeattie in southern Galloway.

heart of the Forest, nearly five miles from the main road. At the end of the minor road which leads to the site stands the four-square Bruce's Stone, a memorial to Robert the Bruce who was (and still is) a popular hero in Galloway since after his victory at Bannockburn in 1314 he gave large tracts of land in the area to his faithful followers.

From this spot a splendid hill-track ascends for over 4 miles to the summit of Merrick (2764 feet), the highest mountain in southern Scotland. The views from the top are superb, with Loch Enoch, just one of a necklace of lochs, glistening a thousand feet below. There are a number of alternative shorter walks in the immediate area, all of them

Below Glen Trool north of Newton Stewart, one of the loveliest parts of Galloway.

exhilarating. Long-distance enthusiasts have a choice of paths networking the whole range between Newton Stewart and New Galloway, with Bargrennan the main starting-point. These routes vary from 15 to 30 miles in length.

The most pleasant return route to Dumfries is along the A712 from Newton Stewart via New Galloway and Crocketford. It runs through grand forest and open moorland, with scarcely any traffic, and passes a number of interesting points, such as Murray's Monument, a lochside deer museum, and a wild goat park. Best of all, though, is the long-disused Old Edinburgh Road which once ran from the capital city to Portpatrick and the Irish ferry. It is now a recognized pedestrian route at its western end for the 18 miles or so from Newton Stewart to New Galloway. In

between (roughly at the half-way mark) is Talnotry and a secluded, though not isolated, Forestry Commission touring-ground by the side of Palnure Burn. The wooded and heather-clad hills which rise to either side approach or exceed the 2000-foot mark and the path skirts picturesque Clatteringshaws Loch as it winds north-east.

To the north stretches the Rhinns of Kells hill range, with Corserine dominating the long ridge at 2669 feet. The most direct ascent route for this grand and isolated string of peaks is from the east. Leave the A713 Dalry to Carsphairn road 2 miles north of Dalry and take the minor road running west up the valley of Polharrow Burn. A track leads from the end of the public road through forest to Loch Harrow and on over North Gairy Top to Corserine.

The Trossachs

Loch Lomond begins just north of Dumbarton where the urban congestion of Glasgow ends. This is the pre-eminent route for most first-time visitors on their way to the Highlands. And indeed, Loch Lomond and the Trossachs are an almost obligatory part of any visit to this area of Scotland. Loch Lomond is Britain's largest lake, 24 miles long and 5 miles at its widest point, and it is also Scotland's most famous. On the eastern side of the Loch, Ben Lomond rises to 3192 feet.

There is a strategic Forestry Commission camping-ground 2 miles south of Aberfoyle, and another at Rowardennan, in Queen Elizabeth Forest Park. From the Rowardennan Hotel there is a well-marked footpath to the summit of Ben Lomond. Within a couple of miles the broad ridge of the mountain rises above the forest and the path follows its crest for 2 more miles to the top where there are splendid views of the Grampians and the Argyllshire Hills.

The whole area offers good walking through magnificent scenery, especially around Craig Rostan high above the eastern banks of Loch Lomond, where the West Highland Way winds on its tortuous route for 95 miles from the outskirts of Glasgow to Fort William. This particular stretch, between the village of Drymen and the Rowardennan Hotel, is one of the prettiest and easiest. The next, to Crianlarich, is distinctly rough in parts, especially around the head of Loch Lomond.

For medium-distance walkers there is another delightful route (with the summit of Ben Lomond as an option) over 13 miles of hill country between Rowardennan and Aberfoyle. This path, via Kinlochard, is just one of several well-marked routes in this area of the western Trossachs. It ascends at first through Duke's Pass and then drops down to the string of waters around Loch Achray, the acknowledged heart of the Trossachs. Ben Venue (2393 feet) rises directly behind the Loch.

Just to the north is Ben A'n, a 1500-foot peak, easy to ascend and rewarding the climber with some more sweeping views from the summit. The path starts almost alongside the Trossachs Hotel and climbs steadily through beautiful birchwoods. This whole area is arguably Scotland at her prettiest, and when the sun shines the aspect is indeed sublime.

Ordnance Survey maps: 56, 57, 65–7, 70–80, 82–6

Left Ben Venue, rising behind Loch Achray, is one of the most richly colourful of all the Scottish mountains. rivalling the best of the Lakeland fells.

The Central Highlands

Those who take the high road to the Highlands via the Forth Road Bridge and M90/A90 to Perth and Dunkeld will be rewarded with a wealth of hill country en route: the Cleish Hills and the Lomond Hills, either side of Loch Leven (the Kinross Loch Leven), and the Ochil and Sidlaw ranges south-west and north-east of Perth, are just a few among many. Space precludes their inclusion in this volume, however, and many other delightful Scottish hills must also unfortunately be omitted. In surveying the high country of a land like Scotland it is difficult to know how to be both selective and fair.

There is, however, one mountain cluster near Killin that must be included for those taking the A84 from Stirling to Lochearnhead, and then through Glen Ogle to the shores of Loch Tay. Five miles from Killin, Ben Lawers, the highest mountain in the southern Highlands, rises to 3984 feet, dominating the western side of Loch Tay. A minor road traverses the mountain, coming in a couple of miles to a car park and the start of the footpath ascent. The route follows a well-defined track along the Burn of Edramucky over Ben Ghlas (3740 feet), eventually ascending a further 700 feet to the top of Ben Lawers. The ascent is easy, and only the last few hundred feet

are at all steep. There is a convenient camping-ground at Cruachan, 3½ miles north-west of Killin off the A827.

Pitlochry, alongside Strath Tay, is the tourist gateway to the Highlands, and itself offers a wide variety of entertainments and activities to suit every taste. One of the most interesting features is the unique Fish Pass at the Pitlochry dam, which enables salmon to get to the upper reaches of the river. The countryside around Pitlochry is very lovely, with some beautiful glen scenery, and there are a number of excellent mountain excursions within easy reach.

The three peaks of Beinn a' Ghlo rise above the Pass of Killiecrankie north of Pitlochry to 3670 feet, the highest some nine miles from any main road. Ben Vrackie looms prominent over Pitlochry, and from the summit at 2757 feet there are vistas across the wooded valleys of the Tay and Tummel rivers. The short and easy path begins at the hamlet of Moulin a mile north of the town.

Right Prospect over Loch Tummel from the lofty projecting rock of Queen's View.

Below The river Lochay in the beautiful Glen Lochay near Killin.

Right Loch Linnhe, dominated on its
eastern side by the shoulder of Ben Nevis.

Not far from here is Blair Atholl with its famous castle which was a fortress during the thirteenth century and the traditional home of the Dukes of Atholl. The lowest of the Beinn a' Ghlo group, Carn Liath, is quite easily accessible from Blair Atholl, via the road leading up Glen Fender to Kirkton. The subsequent ascent is some three miles long to the 3193-foot summit. All this is to be found along one of the busiest summer holiday routes in Scotland by those willing to pause and explore.

Visitors who prefer a less busy base might consider Aberfeldy to the southwest, pleasantly situated amid good scenery. There are particularly scenic walks along the banks of the river to the Mains of Grantully. From here, too, it is not far to Ben Lawers again, or a number of other summits in this south-eastern area of the Grampians.

The Great Glen is a massive volcanic rift which virtually cuts Scotland in half from the North Sea to the Atlantic; it is most clearly defined by the string of lochs, Linnhe, Lochy, and Ness. To the east of the Great Glen rise the principal heights of the Grampians. Within their wide compass towers the highest mountain in the British Isles, while the Cairngorm group are only fractionally lower.

This is really wild high country, even savage in parts, in fact like that of Labrador which lies on the same latitude. The climate on top of the Cairngorms and on Ben Nevis is indeed virtually Arctic. The air over this rugged hinterland is not warmed by the Gulf Stream, as is the west coast, and snow can be found in any of the higher corries at almost any month of the year. This Highland country boasts something in excess of 500 summits topping 3000 feet and a dozen over 4000 feet. Most of the higher peaks lie in the Cairngorm range.

From Pitlochry and Blair Atholl the A9 leads via Dalwhinnie, the head of Loch Ericht, and on to Kingussie and Aviemore. While this may be a main trunk road, often carrying a lot of traffic in summer, it climbs to a thousand feet for much of this stretch and to either side the landscape is wild and beautiful. At Aviemore with its Sports and Leisure Centre, now renowned as a Highland resort, high-country enthusiasts turn east on to the A951 Coylumbridge road and the clear water of Loch Morlich. Surrounded by some 12 000 acres of woodland and high ground, Glen More Forest Park has a fine information centre, a spacious camping-ground on the shores of the Loch, a youth hostel, and an adventure training centre run by the Scottish Sports Council. From the camp site alone, there are three forest trails through ancient pine forests fringing the lower slopes of the surrounding mountains, and five longer waymarked trails. The Loch is now an established water for bathers, anglers, and canoeists, and not far away is the Cairngorm Nature Reserve, one of the largest in Europe.

From the Visitor Centre near Loch an Eilean, 3 miles south of Aviemore, there is a nature-trail on which walkers are sometimes lucky enough to spot fauna which are so rare in other parts of Britain, for here is a safe haven for the Golden Eagle, Osprey, Ptarmigan, and Capercaillie. Those taking to the remoter of the high-country tracks in this region stand an equal – and sometimes better – chance of spotting the Wild Cat or even the Pine Marten.

One of the most celebrated hill-treks in the Cairngorms is the 30-mile marathon from Aviemore to Braemar, which runs past Loch Morlich. It climbs steadily from here through the rugged Larig Ghru Pass and down eventually to Braemar. Here the Scottish mountains are at their most regal, and their sternest. This is definitely not terrain for the inexperienced walker alone.

On one side of the scree-scattered pass Ben Macdhui towers to 4300 feet, the highest mountain in the Cairngorms and the second highest in Scotland. On the opposite side Cairn Toul rises to 4241 feet, with Cairn Gorm, which gives the group its name, almost due south of Ben Macdhui, reaching 4084 feet. This is a two-day trek for all except the speediest (and most agile) hill-walkers. There is no problem with wild camping for self-contained backpackers; those travelling lighter may spend the night in strategic bothies such as Sinclair's Hut. The going is quite reasonable for most of the way, but there is a rough stretch around the Pools of Dee on approach to the summit of the Pass. The descent is gradual and glorious, along a choice of tracks beyond the crags of Devil's Point, to the pretty village of Braemar. Larig Ghru may mean 'Gloomy Pass', but under blue skies it offers the walker an exhilarating experience.

Below Loch an Eilean, Loch of the Island, one of the gems of the area, lies secluded amid wooded hills.

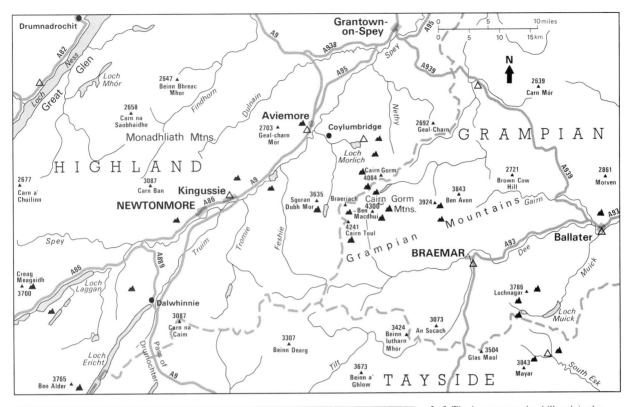

Left The longest one-day hill-trek in the Highlands, from Aviemore to Braemar via the Larig Ghru Pass, runs past Loch Morlich through wild and rugged scenery.

Above The sinister recess of Glen Coe, the Glen of Weeping, the site of the massacre of the Macdonalds by Campbells in 1692.

Not far from Braemar there is another equally spectacular peak, Lochnagar, immortalized by Byron and, latterly, by Prince Charles. It is approached from Ballater along a beautiful minor road on the east side of the Muick to the Spittal of Glen Muick. Here, about a mile from the Loch, a well-walked track climbs westwards away from the glen directly towards the mountain. After a series of zigzags between Meikle Pap and Lochnagar itself, breath-taking views of the north-eastern cliff face are revealed. For those who would press on to the summit at 3786 feet, the path continues south-west following the cliff edges beyond the great corrie at the south-western end.

North-east of the Cairngorms lies one of the largest – and least-trodden – mountain ranges in Britain, the Mon-adhliaths. It is a vast swathe of high country some fifty miles long and half as wide at its broadest, as yet unscarred by a single major road. There is, however, the historic General Wade's Road, a military road built in the eighteenth century to link the Hanoverian strong-hold of Fort Augustus to the north–south communication route, now known as the A9. The old track skirts the southern massif of the Monadhliath Mountains; there is easy access from the hamlet of Laggan Bridge, south-west of Aviemore, via the A9 and A86. From here, a minor road leads to Garva Bridge and runs into the track which climbs over the summit of Corrieyairack Pass (2507 feet), the scenic climax of this 18-mile route which is wild and distinctly remote, even today. The fort at Fort Augustus, incidentally,

is now an Abbey and open to visitors. It was one of a chain of defensive bastions below Loch Ness, of which Fort William was the principal.

Contemporary Fort William (which has become geared to tourism in recent years) is the accepted crossroads of the Highlands. Now a resort of high standing with every conceivable facility, it also lies strategically as a base for exploring the most dramatic of the Grampians which are a magnet for climbers and hill-walkers the world over. Ben Nevis, Britain's highest mountain, is just one target among many.

The southern approach route – and the most visually exciting – begins a dozen miles south-west (as the crow flies, three times that distance via man-made roads) at the western end of Rannoch Moor. Here the A82 leaves the landscape of heather and lochs to enter Glen Coe, the Glen of Weeping. Even though dissected by the new main road, the mighty canyon still conveys a magic aura of grandeur and poignant history. At times, when the dark clouds are scudding, the deeper recesses of this dark ravine are palpably awesome.

Climbers and the more tigerish hill-walkers are here offered a wealth, almost a surfeit, of towering rock faces, the most challenging of buttresses, and razor-edge ridges to tempt all those who have ever felt the pull of the vertical sport. Here, too, is one of the principal mountaineering centres in Scotland and latterly, in winter, a ski-resort with a chair-lift for those who prefer the easy way up and the quick way down.

Above The recognized, and regal, approach to Ben Nevis is along the road and footpath through Glen Nevis.

The eastern guardian of the Glen Coe peaks is Buachaille Etive Mor (The Great Shepherd of Etive), towering to 3345 feet. On the north side is the long ridge of the Aonach Eagach (3168 feet), and on the south the great spurs of Bidean nam Bian (3766 feet). These three mountains have the reputation of being more formidable than anything further south and there are no easy walking routes to their respective summits. It seems almost unnecessary to add that the novice should not attempt these slopes unless in the company of experienced walkers, though the figures of accidents in the area indicate that such a warning must be repeated.

There is, however, a relatively easy route to the higher shoulder of The Great Shepherd which begins just off the A82, 2½ miles west of Kingshouse Hotel. From here a minor road and track winds in an ascent around the mountain to reach the main ridge. Even if you do not achieve the summit (from where there are fine anticipatory views of the squat Ben Nevis group), this is a walk on the wild side and splendidly exhilarating.

Glen Coe has a Visitor Information Centre, ample car parking, and limited free camping space for bona-fide climbers and hill-walkers. There is also a Forestry Commission touring-ground, 2 miles east of Glencoe village, in a spectacular setting just off the A82 and close to the scene of the 1692 Massacre.

Ballachulish, along the road from Glencoe, now linked to Fort William by bridge, also has a first-rate information centre to help newcomers make the most of the region. Pause here, if only to take in the view westwards of the gigantic mountain mass now dominated by the distinctive Pap of Glencoe. Here, beside Linnhe, the great sea-loch, there is a choice of routes to Fort William. First-timers may prefer the longer route around Loch Leven, for this encircling stretch of the A82 is distinctly free of traffic since the demise of the old ferry.

Fort William offers a wide choice of accommodation, of all standards, both within the town itself and in the surrounding area. One possibility for the camper is the touring site set in the beautiful Glen Nevis. The view of Ben Nevis from Fort William is not particularly dramatic, and in fact there is just a tantalizing glimpse of the mighty shoulder. For a distant view of the summit it is necessary to take the A82 for a mile or so northwards.

To see the mountain at close quarters,

however, you could scarcely be better based. A short drive along the Glen to The Falls and beyond on a single-track road, then by footpath, guarantees a singular experience. This is the recognized route to the summit at 4406 feet, and the path is well marked and well trodden, especially on the lower slopes. As the time needed for the full ascent is usually some four hours, pedestrian traffic thins appreciably at the higher altitudes. Ben Nevis is not a difficult mountain to climb and stamina rather

than agility is the prime requirement. The path traverses the face of Meall an t-Suidhe (Hill of Rest), then crosses over to the main shoulder. On the celebrated summit there is the remains of an observatory built in 1883 and on a clear day you can see from the Isle of Jura to the Cairngorms. At the northern edge there are the gigantic cliffs and gullies dropping away from the sky-scraper plateau, the highest in the British Isles.

This is just one of several routes (the north-east scarp probably offers the best

of Ben Nevis to the climber), but these others are strictly for the experienced and in fine weather conditions. Even then care is needed, especially in the vicinity of snow cornices that crown the gullies around the perimeter edge of the great plateau.

To the south of Glen Nevis there are also the Mamore Mountains, two of which, Stob Ban (3274 feet), and Sgurr a' Mhaim (3600 feet), are accessible to walkers from the farm-track at Achria-bhach, 6 miles along the Glen from Fort

William. The West Highland Way skirts the western slopes of the Mamores on its final leg before entering Glen Nevis just below the Ben. It is said that walkers of the West Highland Way are recognized by their skeletal frames, wild eyes, and bulging calves. This is only half the truth, however. They also have a tangibly triumphant bearing, and a store of memories beyond price.

Ordnance Survey maps: 26, 34–6, 41–3, 50–3

Above left Sgurr a' Mhaim in the beautiful Glen Nevis, a scenic gorge of tree-hung rock bluffs.

Above The route around Loch Leven offers a splendid approach to Fort William through spectacular scenery.

The Western Highlands and Skye

The main tourist route north – the 'romantic' route, it may be called – from Glasgow on the A82 along Loch Lomondside may be picturesque, but the road is winding, narrow, and it does suffer a degree of congestion in the summer. A classic alternative approach to the Western Highlands on the far side of the Great Glen is to take the A814 via Helensburgh, alongside Clydeside, Gare Loch, and Loch Long.

The first scenic delight en route is The Cobbler, one of Scotland's most distinctive mountains, and the best known of the Arrochar Alps which stand at the head of Loch Long. Though not the highest mountain in this range, The Cobbler rises to 2891 feet above the shores of Loch Long. Its weird three-peak configuration is served by an easy ascent path via Buttermilk Burn close to the Forestry Commission camping-ground at Ardgartan. Ben Ime, the highest of this group at 3318 feet, is also accessible from this path.

The A83 through Glen Croe, now modernized and graded, flirts sporadically with that marvellous and tortuous road of old, the 'Rest and be Thankful', the scene of countless exciting hill-climbing events. Landscape beauty on the grand scale continues all the way to Inverary around the head of Loch Fyne. On the west bank of the Aray river stands Inverary Castle, ancestral home of the Dukes of Argyll since the fifteenth century. Inverary is an attractive town, set against a background of wooded hills with the clear waters of the Loch in front. Despite its position on the Highland road, Inverary has escaped the worst ravages of tourism. The Highland road doubles back on itself here, but a glance at the map will show why.

A fine run north through Glen Aray follows to the head of Loch Awe, where the visitor is faced with a choice of routes: to turn east and then north for Glen Coe and Fort William; or west and north via Oban and Loch Linnhe. Both routes are beautiful, both pass through memorable high country.

The first alternative follows the A85 which winds between Dalmally and Tyndrum alongside Loch Lochy. There are fine mountains south-east of here, most of them topping 3000 feet, one of the most dramatic being Cruach Ardrain. The best approach is from Crianlarich, where the path begins about half a mile south from the village, ascending through wooded slopes to the high north-west ridge and 3428-foot summit.

Left The old 'Rest and be Thankful' road runs through the wild and rugged Glen Croe. It takes its name from the inscription on a stone set beside the road at the top of the Glen.

Right The ruined Kilchurn Castle, set on a peninsula at the foot of Loch Awe. The Pass of Brander and Ben Cruachan rise to the north of the loch.

Below Glen Etive stretches from the northern end of Loch Etive in the heart of the Western Highlands.

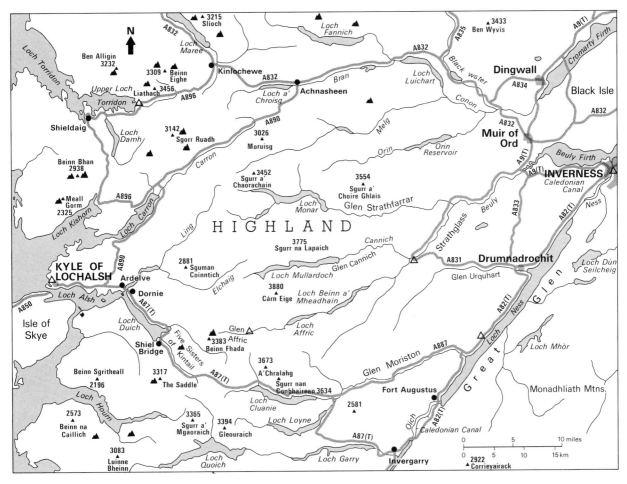

Map labels:

N

Loch Torridon
A832
▲ 3215 Slioch
Loch Fannich
Loch Maree
▲ 3433 Ben Wyvis
A9(T)
Cromarty Firth
A835
Ben Alligin 3232
A832
3309 ▲ ▲ Beinn Eighe
Kinlochewe
A832
Bran
Loch Luichart
Dingwall
A834
Black Isle
Upper Loch Liathach 3456
A896
Loch a' Chroisg
Achnasheen
A890
Loch water
Muir of Ord
A832
A87(T)
A832
Torridon
Shieldaig
Loch Damh
3142 Sgorr Ruadh
3026 Moruisg
Melg
Orin
Orin Reservoir
INVERNESS
Caledonian Canal
Beuly Firth
A9(T)
Beinn Bhan 2938
A896
▲ 3452 Sgurr a' Chaorachain
3554 Sgurr a' Choire Ghlais
Glen Strathfarrar
Beuly
A833
Ness
Meall Gorm 2325
Loch Kishorn
Loch Carron
Carron
Ling
Loch Monar
Strathglass
HIGHLAND
3775 Sgurr na Lapaich
Cannich
Drumnadrochit
A831
Loch Dùn Seilcheig
KYLE OF LOCHALSH
A890
Ardelve
2881 ▲ Sguman Coinntich
Elchaig
Loch Mullardoch
Glen Cannich
Glen Urquhart
Ness
Glen
Dornie
A87(T)
3880 Càrn Eige
Loch Beinn a' Mheadhain
Loch Alsh
Isle of Skye
Loch Duich
Loch Affric
A82(T)
Loch Mhòr
Five Sisters of Kintail
Glen ▲ Affric
Shiel Bridge
3383 Beinn Fhada
3673 A'Chralahg
A887
Loch
Beinn Sgritheall 2196
3317 The Saddle
A87(T)
Sgurr nan Conbhairean 3634
Glen Moriston
Fort Augustus
Monadhliath Mtns.
Loch Hourn
2573 Beinn na Caillich
3365 Sgurr a' Mgaoraich
3394 Gleouraich
Loch Cluanie
Loch Loyne
2581
Caledonian Canal
Oich
3083 Luinne Bheinn
Loch Quoich
Loch Garry
A87(T)
Invergarry
Great Glen
0   5   10 miles
0   5   10   15 km
2922 ▲ Corrieyairack

Ben More is the dominant peak of the cluster at an elevation of 3843 feet; Ben Lui (3708 feet) to the west is best tackled from the Glen Lochy road, roughly half-way between Dalmally and Tyndrum, where there is a river footbridge. From Tyndrum, the road is high and handsome, a terrain of sweeping wide vistas, with the great Grampian massif on the northern horizon and Glen Coe beyond.

Back at Dalmally, those opting for the majestic splintered seaboard of the Highlands begin their western approach with an equally impressive sight: the Pass of Brander and that now singular mountain Ben Cruachan. Singular, since this giant, sandwiched between Loch Awe and Loch Etive, has been cunningly hollowed out to house a huge hydro-electric plant (open to visitors). Cruachan, towering to 3689 feet, is just one of a regal group commanding the heights of the Brander Pass. To the south of the mountain an access road runs through Allt Cruachan corrie to the hydro reservoir. From here it is a mile or

so walk north-west via Meall Cuanail Col to the summit and a superb pre-view of the sea-loch terrain ahead.

It is not obligatory to detour south-west from Connel Bridge to Oban, though surely no one would bypass it knowingly, despite the persistent pull of the far north-west. It is worth pausing amid lusher, sea-level landscape in one of Scotland's most intriguing places. Known once, for some obscure reason, as the Charing Cross of the Highlands, the dominating landmark of Oban is a wildly misplaced replica of the Colosseum at Rome, a folly erected by an eccentric nineteenth-century banker called McCaig. Oban is a comfortable holiday resort, offering a wide choice of accommodation, and is a splendid centre from which to tour the Western Highlands.

Within easy reach of the town there are such varied attractions as the cliff edges of the Firth of Lorn; the gaunt thirteenth-century ruins of Dunstaffnage Castle where Flora Macdonald was incarcerated for helping Prince Charlie

in 1745; and the swift Falls of Lorca spilling from Loch Etive into Ardmucknish Bay. For the self-contained tourist there is a pleasant farm camping-ground in a hill-top setting near Gallanach, 2½ miles from Oban.

The immediate magnet for walkers is the little island of Kerrera lying seductively below in the Sound, reached by a foot-passenger ferry. The views from the west shores of the island are splendid, extending south beyond Jura and Colonsay to the open Atlantic and north to the start of the Great Glen.

From Oban the A828 leads north around Benderloch to Ballachulish and on to Fort William and Fort Augustus on the A82. Here the main road switches from the eastern to the western flank of the Great Glen. The direct route north (the A82) follows the shores of Loch Ness to Inverness, but the visitor in search of exhilarating high country can turn off on to the A831 at Drummna-drochit for Glen Affric and Glen Cannich, two of the most beautiful glens in the Highlands. The approach, along

Below Glen Shiel, at the head of Loch Duich, lies on the main route to the Western ranges and Skye.

Opposite View towards Glen Affric and the central Highlands from the west.

Glen Urquhart, is through magnificent woodland to the glittering string of lochs which grace these glens.

For walkers and climbers the prospects are as wide as could be wished. One recognized route through these magnificent hills is from Glen Affric to Loch Duich. Cars must be left at the western end of Loch Beneveian, from where a forestry road and track winds along loch shore and river to the youth hostel at Alltbeath. From here, the track skirts the northern slopes of the famous Five Sisters of Kintail and finishes after 18 miles at Croe Bridge on Loch Duich.

From Loch Beneveian another hill-track leads to Carn Eige and Mam Soul, the highest mountains in the Western Highlands, both exceeding 3800 feet and both well away from access roads. Because of this comparative isolation it is only strong walkers who will attempt both ascent and descent in one day. The track is reached from the car park, with a subsequent long, but rewarding, ascent

via Gleann nam Fiadh.

Those who choose to continue to Inverness and on westwards to Loch Maree, will find themselves on one of the most regal routes in northern Britain. Through tiny Achnasheen and down to Kinlochewe the road climbs skywards and swoops through seemingly endless beauty. Some five miles from Kinlochewe, Slioch seems to rise directly from the waters of the Loch to a height of 3217 feet. There is a good path to the summit from the head of the Loch up Glen Bannisdail. Access is free at all times except during the deer-stalking season. From Loch Maree it is but a short distance to the Torridons and Gairloch.

The alternative, classic, approach to the Western ranges, however, is via the A87, west from Invergarry. The road winds through Glen Garry, Glen Shiel, and alongside Loch Duich. Here there are more grand mountains, especially on the northern side of Loch Cluanie. The

Above The majestic peaks of the Five Sisters of Kintail rise above Glen Shiel beyond Loch Duich.

Opposite The broad shoulders of Slioch dominate the beautiful sweep of Loch Maree.

principal peaks are A'Chralaig and Sgurr nan Conbhairean, both over 3600 feet. There is a recognized track to A'Chralaig leading off the tarmac road at the western end of the Loch near the Cluanie Hotel; the track to Sgurr nan Conbhairean begins 3 miles east of the inn, a direct if fairly easy ascent up the south slope.

From Glen Shiel, further along the A87, there is access to the Five Sisters of Kintail, another majestic mountain mass topped by Sgurr Fhuaran (3505 feet). The most popular and direct ascent of this peak is via the western ridge from a track which starts a mile and a half upriver from Shiel Bridge. Though not difficult, it is an unrelieved uphill haul all the way to the summit. There is a convenient camping-ground for the region at Ardelve, north-west of Dornie.

Just west of Dornie lie Loch Alsh, the Kyle of Lochalsh, and the ferry to Skye.

Before crossing that narrow strip of water, however, there is one more mainland route so grandiose that it must be taken first. This is the A890 and A896 which circles Loch Carron then switches west and north to Shieldaig and Loch Torridon. This stretch is equally beautiful in both directions, from the Kyle northwards, or from the popular entry route to Wester Ross via the A832. This road snakes through Achnasheen and Kinlochewe and then along the huge and enchanting expanse of Loch Maree. There is a superb touring holiday centre just west of Gairloch, in a setting which combines undulating green hills and sand-dunes, a golden beach, gin-clear water, and seascapes across the Hebrides and Skye. Just one excursion by car and on foot from this centre is around Gair Loch through Badacro to Red Point and then on foot to Diabeg along the shores of Loch Torridon.

At the head of Loch Torridon, the walker or climber is in a perfect position to explore some of the most majestic of the heights of the Torridons, mountains of fascinating character, and some of the finest in Scotland. These are great blocks of sandstone and contrasting quartzite, not so much a range of individual summits as a complexity of clustered peaks, corries, and ridges.

Ben Alligin, topping 3232 feet, is one of the most popular with first-timers, since it is easier to scale than neighbouring Liathach (3456 feet), or the giant Beinn Eighe (3309 feet), the easternmost of this particular trio. The best route for Ben Alligin starts some two miles west of the village of Torridon and winds north-west then north via open hill and corrie to the southern slope of the mountain. Some care is needed in picking the right track after the Sgurr Mor ridge to avoid scrambling, but once the Horns of Alligin are traversed, the descent south-east is easy, via a well-trodden corrie path down to the lochside. The other two mountains are really the province of expert climbers or *very* experienced walkers ready to use their hands on the trickier traverses.

The scenery of the Torridons is so spectacular that even if you only set foot on the lowest and most modest slope, some of the magic of the landscape will surely rub off. It is a world of wild mountains, pine forests, shimmering lochs, and the priceless silence which still prevails in this remote corner of the British Isles. There is a small camping-ground at Inverewe, next to the famous Inverewe Gardens.

High-country excitement of a different kind is offered by the drive to Apple-cross, a journey along one of the highest roads in Britain, combining both scenic and driving thrills in one. Only a few years ago Applecross was the most inaccessible village on Britain's mainland. From Gairloch, make for Kinlochewe, then turn west through Glen Torridon along the southern shore of Upper Loch Torridon to Shieldaig where there is a small camping-ground above the Loch.

The new road continues around the head of Loch Torridon. If you are sharp-eyed and attentive, you may spot Sea Otters in any of the waters in this vicinity. Applecross is a tiny hamlet of just one street boasting a post office, a pub, and a camping-ground on the splendid headland plateau. One pleasant scenic surprise is the opulent growth of trees and lush green, after the stark heights of the mountain road. The views across the Inner Sound to Raasay and Rona, with Skye beckoning beyond, are unbelievably dramatic in certain lights, while the sunsets are pure magic.

If the road from Shieldaig was wild and remote, then the 17-mile stretch back to the A896 at Loch Kishorn is even more of a challenge. This sky-scraper twisting road is the once-notorious Bealach na Ba, Pass of the Cattle. One of the highest roads in Great Britain, it rises through a series of dramatic hairpins – some of them 1 in 4 – to pass between Sgurr a Chaorachain (2539 feet) and Meall Gorm (2325 feet). A notice by the Applecross camping-ground warns that this road is unsuitable for caravans. There are really no difficulties, however, for the proficient driver at the wheel of a well-matched outfit, at least during the summer.

Right Upper Loch Torridon. The area is rich in spectacular and exciting mountain heights.

Skye

This circuit of the major Highland mountain ranges on the mainland has of necessity been selective, and apologies are due to those devotees whose personal favourites lie in the far north above Ullapool or around Cape Wrath, or on the offshore islands of Arran in the south or Harris in the Outer Hebrides.

One final area which must be included, however, since it boasts some of the most sheer-sided and rockiest mountains in the British Isles, is the Island of Skye. The crossing by ferry takes less than ten minutes, but it is a step into what seems almost another land. For here is an island leaning back on 2000 years of independent history and, though only 50 miles long with a width varying between 4 and 25 miles, it has a coastline of almost 900 miles, most of which is scarcely populated. Above all, Skye has the Cuillin Hills.

Most visitors make for Portree, the capital of the island, via Broadford, which has a good tourist information office. The first of Skye's spectacular mountain ranges, the Red Hills, forms a backdrop to the village, and further along stands the Sligachan Hotel, a much-favoured starting-point for excursions into the Cuillins. There is a well-marked route west of the Hotel to the summit of Sgurr nan Gillean (3167 feet), the most prominent peak of the northern range.

There is no rule, though, which states that you *must* reach the summit, and indeed, it should be stressed that few of the peaks can be reached without scrambling, that magnetic compasses are not always reliable on Skye, and that thick cloud can descend very quickly. It cannot be emphasized too strongly that walking and climbing in these hills are dangerous for those unaccustomed to such conditions and should not be undertaken by the inexperienced. Touring sites are mainly small, intimate, and simply part of working farms.

The northern part of Skye is still largely crofting country and the scenery all the way to the tip of the island is consistently dramatic. The Old Man of Storr is just one distinctive highlight in this landscape of basalt blended with sandstone and limestone. This weird pinnacle lies some six miles from Portree and dominates the steep cliffs which rise sheer to 2360 feet.

Left The Cuillins, seen here from Sligachan, are considered by many to be among the most spectacular heights in Britain.

Below The Old Man of Storr, an extraordinary rock pinnacle atop sheer cliffs north of Portree.

Staffin, a scattered settlement of small-holdings, nestles in a beautiful bay on the slopes at the foot of the Quiraing Rocks, a cluster of needle-point cliffs and peaks of strange and fascinating formations. The paths up the mountain are narrow and care must be taken in the vicinity of the distinctive scallop known as The Prison. North-western Skye has another famous landmark, Dunvegan Castle, the ancient seat of the Clan Macleod chiefs, in a regal setting on the shore of the Loch. At nearby Dunvegan Head there are the highest of Skye's sea-cliffs. There are two touring sites here and the village shops are well stocked. For a fine coral beach, take the minor road north from Dunvegan to Claigan. The sunsets are frequently of incredible beauty.

The Cuillins, which rise in the west of the island, are ranked as the most spectacular heights in Britain. Their composition is mainly of gabbro, coarse-grained black rock very different from the granite of the neighbouring Red Hills. Erosion by ice has plucked out the gabbro crystals, forming steep-walled corries, vast scree slopes, and extensive areas of clean rough rock. The famous Cuillin ridge forms a horseshoe around Loch Coruisk and although the highest peak (Sgurr Alasdair) only reaches 3309 feet, the awesome steepness of the hills rising from so close to the sea makes them appear much higher. For most hill-walkers and climbers it is almost a religious experience simply to stand and survey them.

Glen Brittle, at the foot of the Cuillins, is an ideal base from which to make forays into the hills. There is a youth hostel, and a large camping-ground on the shores of Loch Brittle. The resident wardens at the site also provide instruction in mountaineering techniques. And indeed, it is with this necessary combination of enthusiasm and expertise that walkers and climbers come from all over the world to enjoy the magnificent splendour of this area of upland Britain.

Ordnance Survey maps: 19, 20, 23–6, 32–5, 40–2

Above The dramatic summit ridge of Blaven (3042 feet) from Torrin.

Right The cliffs and pinnacles of Quiraing form one of the strangest and most fascinating mountains in Scotland.

Safety First

There are no legal constraints on the walker to take care of himself in remote hill country, and no law can stop you if you want to behave with suicidal rashness. You are, however, under a moral obligation to avoid putting your potential rescuers at unnecessary risk, which is reason enough to take all reasonable precautions.

Never set out into unknown terrain on a whim; make sure that every expedition is properly prepared. Do not walk alone until you are both experienced and confident, are proficient with map and compass, and know your own limitations.

Walking alone away from recognized, frequented footpaths can nevertheless be hazardous. It is pleasant to walk in the company of another person, and a third person is even better: in case of accident, one can stay with the injured person while the other goes for help.

There is no need to be timid or inflexible, however. A walk on the Chilterns in summer is obviously quite different from an ascent of Great Gable in winter, as you will soon discover. A sensible rule is to err on the side of caution. Never under-estimate any high terrain, however friendly it may seem in sunshine, and always be prepared for the worst. At high altitudes the weather can change with alarming rapidity. Mid-winter conditions can prevail on the summit of Snowdon or Ben Nevis even at the height of summer.

Distances can be deceptive in high country, and a long and tiring walk may be needed to reach a road or habitation that appears only a short way off. And remember that once your energy begins to drain, it does so very quickly. This makes it all the more vital to have the right clothing and equipment, wayfinding skill, and knowledge of how to act in an emergency.

Never set off on a mountain expedition without informing someone of your destination and when you intend to return. Even a note taped to the inside of your car windscreen is better than nothing, though it is obviously more advisable to notify a park warden, the police, or a person at your base.

Always carry the standard emergency survival gear: extra warm clothing, means of providing a hot drink, fast-energy food such as chocolate, a first-aid kit, torch, and whistle. Memorize the standard distress warning in the hills, six flashes or whistle blasts.

If you should find yourself in real trouble, either through injury or exhaustion, then stop, take stock, and take action. There are 200 deaths in Britain's mountains each year, and most of them are caused by exposure, made worse by ignorance or fear. It is perhaps fear that is the greatest killer simply because fear makes people virtually unable to think straight or take the right actions.

The natural inclination, which is sometimes hard to resist, is to rush down the mountain regardless. This is the very worst thing you could do. Stay where you are, sheltered from the wind in a nest of bracken if possible. Put on all the clothes you have, including waterproofs, eat some of your rations, and wait for help to arrive. The thought that someone will come to your aid should help to sustain you and keep fear at bay.

It is fortunately only a very small minority of people who get into really serious trouble, and it is worth bearing this in mind. Behave in a sensible and responsible fashion, and you should enjoy a lifetime of high-country exploration.

Walking Within the Law

The walker's legal obligations are few, simple, straightforward, and mainly common sense. You have the legal right to walk on the 100 000 and more miles of public footpaths in Britain. If these paths are also bridleways, you may cycle along them or ride on a horse.

Your rights apply only to the actual path or bridleway and not to adjacent land, whether fenced or open. Every square foot of the country is owned by an individual or a public authority; there is no such thing as 'common' land. Even though a path crosses remote wild country, the walker does not have free access to camp, light fires, pick flowers, or leave rubbish. This is important on fells and open moorland, and crucial in farmland and forests.

Do not ignore 'keep closed' notices

on farm gates, even if animals are not in view. To let your dog chase sheep is indictable, but in hill-farm country farmers may respond with a shot-gun.

Not all paths are clearly signposted, and you may sometimes come upon a tangle of undergrowth or a field of corn where the map indicates a path. On this point the law is both complex and uncertain. A landowner is obliged by law to keep public rights of way clear of obstructions; if he does not cut back undergrowth the local authority is empowered to do so and charge him for the service. The case is similar with fields of wheat. Provided he has given prior notice, a farmer may in some cases sow or plough over a path, so long as he restores the right of way within a specified time.

If a path definitely does pass through a field of wheat, you may follow it, making sure you cause as little damage as possible. In practice, few people have the courage to do this, but by making a detour, perhaps round the edge of the field, they commit trespass. The only answer in such situations is to use intelligence and care, and to avoid any outright confrontation.

Some obstructions, such as bulls, pose a more difficult problem. Local bye-laws do vary, and it is sometimes necessary for a farmer to graze bulls on land crossed by recognized footpaths, and notices are not always displayed. Take sensible precautions and be alert at all times, ensuring that children and elderly people do not walk near the animal.

The Country Code

All country walkers should abide by the Country Code. Its few rules are simple, and by rigidly observing them we help to preserve the countryside and an atmosphere of trust between town and country dwellers.

Guard against all risk of fire
A carelessly thrown match or cigarette-end could start an inferno, especially in forests at dry seasons. Never light a cooking fire when camping without express permission to do so.

Fasten all gates
This should be automatic; even if you find a farm gate open, close it behind you. It can take hours to recover a straying animal which can damage itself or growing crops or cause a serious road accident.

Keep dogs under control
Dogs should be put on a lead whenever requested and always when crossing sheep-grazing land and during the lambing season. A wayward dog almost always signifies an irresponsible owner. Make sure both you and your pet are properly trained to wander the countryside.

Keep to rights of way across farmland
Crops are valuable and are not always instantly identifiable as such: what may look like grass may be precious clover or young wheat.

Avoid damaging fences, hedges, and walls
If you do have to force your way through a fence or hedge, do so as delicately as possible. If you inadvertently dislodge a dry-stone wall in hill country, repair it before moving on.

Leave no litter
This is a slovenly, unsociable, and dangerous habit. Plastic bags choke cattle and tin cans and bottles will slash paws, hooves, and tendons. Take your litter home with you or to a litter basket.

Safeguard water supplies
Never pollute flowing streams with waste matter or detergent. All our drinking water comes from country streams and reservoirs, so keep them pure.

Protect wild life, plants, and trees
The ecology of the countryside is delicately balanced. Do not disturb the fine interweave of animal and plant life by picking flowers, uprooting trees, or killing or frightening wild creatures.

Go carefully on country roads
These are working routes for farmers. If a tractor or a flock of sheep blocks your way or slows you down, show patience and courtesy: you are the interloper.

Respect the life of the countryside
For the countryman, the landscape is an open-air workshop, and farm machinery and implements are often left unattended. Allay the traditional suspicion of country people for town dwellers by considerate and responsible behaviour.

Mountaineering Courses

The following is a shortened list of organizations and centres which run courses in mountaineering and kindred activities in Britain. Brief details of the types of courses offered, their duration, and the age groups accepted are given, but full information should be obtained from the individual organizations.

ENGLAND

Allenheads Outdoor Education Centre
Allenheads, Hexham, Northumberland
Mountaineering, walking, rock-climbing, skiing, mountain rescue.
Week-end and week; normally schools; 10 years min.
Closed in school holidays.

Catton Field Study and Expedition Centre
Allendale, Hexham, Northumberland
All courses and field study.
Week-end and week; generally schools; 10 years min.
Open all year.

Dukeshouse Wood Centre
Hexham, Northumberland
Walking, rock-climbing, orienteering.
Week-end, week, and longer; not open to public;
10 years min.
Open March–December.

Allenheads Lodge Outdoor Activity Centre
Dovespool, Allenheads, Northumberland
Mountaineering, walking, rock-climbing, skiing.
Week-end and week; open to public, youth, schools;
12 years min.
Open all year.

Stainsacre Hall
Stainsacre, Whitby, Yorkshire
Mountaineering, walking.
Week-end and week; open to public; 18 years min.
Open all year.

Hollowford Training Centre
Castleton, Sheffield
Mountaineering, walking, rock-climbing, caving.
Week-end, week, and longer; open to public; no age limit.
Open all year.

Whitehall Centre for Open Country Pursuits
Long Hill, Buxton, Derbyshire
Mountaineering, walking, rock-climbing.
Week-end and week; open to public; 16 years min.
Open all year.

Glenbrook Outdoor Activities Training Centre
Bamford, Sheffield
Walking, rock-climbing, caving, etc.
Week-end and week; open to members of Girl Guides and Scout Associations; 14 years min.
Open all year.

Stanley Head Outdoor Pursuits Centre
Tompkin Lane, Stanley, Stockton Brook, Stoke-on-Trent
Mountaineering, walking, rock-climbing.
Day, week-end, and week; Stoke-on-Trent schools only; no age limit.
Open all year.

North Pennine Outdoor Pursuits
King's Court, Pateley Bridge, Harrogate, North Yorkshire
Walking, climbing, caving, sailing, skiing, pony-trekking, orienteering, canoeing.
Week-end and week; open to public; 17 years min.
(unless with family).

Biberry Hill Training Centre
Rose Hill, Belnall, Birmingham
Orienteering and adventure.
Week-end; open to Birmingham clubs but special courses arranged for any organization; 14 years min.
Open all year.

Woodlands Outdoor Centre
Glasbury-on-Wye, via Hereford
Mountaineering, rock-climbing, caving.
Week, 2 weeks, and longer; open to educational organizations, clubs; 13 years min.
Closed during August.

Youth Adventure Centre
The Court House, Longtown, Hereford
Mountaineering, walking, rock-climbing, dry-skiing, rescue, etc.
Week-end, week, and 2 weeks; open to public during school holidays, otherwise schools only; 14-21 years.
Open all year.

Poole and Dorset Adventure Centre
Hercules Road, Hamworthy, Poole, Dorset
Rock-climbing, expedition camping.
Week; open to schools, youth service, and industry;
14 years min.
Open February–November.

Youth Activities Centre
Knightsdale Road, Weymouth, Dorset
Mountaineering, rock-climbing, cliff rescue.
About 12 days; open to public; 14–23 years.
Open all year.

ELE Ltd
Ilkley, West Yorkshire
Walking, canoeing, caving, rock-climbing, orienteering.
Week-end and week; open to public.

Drake's Island
Millbay Dock, Plymouth
Rock-climbing.
Week-end and week; open to public; 12½ years min.
Open March–October.

Pixies Holt Residential Youth Centre
Pixies Holt, Dartmeet, Devon
Walking, rock-climbing.
Duration as requested; open to public;
14 years min.
Open all year.

Bowles Outdoor Pursuits Centre
Sandhill Lane, Eridge, Tunbridge Wells, Kent
Rock-climbing, skiing.
Week-end and week; open to public, colleges, etc.;
15 years min. (unless block-booking with leader in attendance).
Open all year.

Burwash Place Outdoor Centre
Etchingham, Sussex
Rock-climbing, expeditions, field study.
Week-end and week; mainly Brighton LEA;
13 years min.
Open all year.

Crowden Outdoor Centre
Hadfield, Hyde, Cheshire
Walking, rock-climbing, caving.
Open to public; 18 years min.
Open all year.

Oldham College of Technology
Rochdale Road, Oldham, Lancashire
Mountaineering, walking, climbing, skiing, caving.

Climbing and Adventure Holidays
Rowland Edwards, Compass West, Sunny Corner
Lane, Sennen, Cornwall
Expert tuition with a professional guide.

Mountain Experience
12 Piershill Terrace, Edinburgh
Overseas expeditions and UK courses.

LAKE DISTRICT
Thurston Outdoor Activity Centre
Thurston, Coniston, Cumbria
Mountaineering, walking, rock-climbing.
Day, week-end, week, 12 days; not open to public;
13 years min.
Open all year.

Outward Bound Mountain School
Ullswater, nr. Penrith, Cumbria
Mountaineering, walking, rock-climbing, skiing,
mountain rescue.
Day, week-end, week, 26-day Outward Bound
Courses; open to public; 10 years min.
Open all year.

Howtown Outdoor Activity Centre
Ullswater, nr. Penrith, Cumbria
Mountaineering, walking, rock-climbing, skiing.
Some courses open to public; 13 years min.
Open all year.

Whernside Manor
Dent, Sedbergh, Cumbria
Caving, walking, weather lore.
Week-end, week, and longer; open to public.

YMCA National Training Centre
Lakeside, Ulverston, Lancashire
Mountaineering, walking, rock-climbing.
Week-end, week, and longer; open to public; schools,
youth groups, colleges, industry; 11 years min.
Open all year.

Outward Bound School
Eskdale Green, Holmbrook, Cumbria
Mountaineering, walking, rock-climbing,
mountain rescue.
No short courses; open to public; 16 years min.
Open all year.

Brathay Hall
Ambleside, Cumbria
Mountaineering, walking.
No short courses; not open to public; 17–21 years.
Open all year.

High Level Mountain Camping
Klets, Seathwaite, Broughton-in-Furness, Cumbria
Duration 1800 hours Monday–1700 hours Friday;
min. number for each holiday 4, max. 8.

NORTH WALES
Nant Bwlch y Haearn Outdoor Pursuits Centre
Nant Bwlch yr Haearn, Llanrwst, Clwyd
Mountaineering, walking, rock-climbing,
mountain rescue, skiing, etc.
Week-end, week, and longer; Clywd LEA users;
14 years min.
Open all year.

Plas Gwynant Outdoor Education Centre
Nant Gwynant, Gwynedd
Mountaineering, walking, rock-climbing, etc.
Week-end, week, 11 days.
Open all year.

**Wolverhampton Education Committee Outdoor
Pursuits Centre**
The Towers, Capel Curig, Betws-y-Coed, Gwynedd
Mountaineering, hill-walking, rock-climbing, etc.
Week-end and week; Wolverhampton parties only;
14 years min.
Open all year.

Llanrug Outdoor Activities Centre
Llanrug, Gwynedd
Mountaineering, walking, rock-climbing,
mountain rescue.
Week-end, week, and longer; Worcester County
schools and employees only; 13 years min.
Open all year.

Ogwen Cottage Outdoor Pursuits Centre
Bethesda, nr. Bangor, Gwynedd
Mountaineering, walking, rock-climbing, skiing,
mountain rescue.
Week and 12 days; Birmingham LEA only;
14 years min.
Open during school term.

Cobdens Snowdonia Club
Capel Curig, Betws-y-Coed, Gwynedd
Walking, rock-climbing, orienteering.
Open to public.
Open 15 October–1 May.

Kent Mountain Centre
Glyn Padarn, Llanberis, Gwynedd
Mountaineering, walking, rock-climbing.
Week; not open to public (Kent county only);
no age limit.
Open all year.

Plas y Brenin, National Mountaineering Centre
Capel Curig, Betws-y-Coed, Gwynedd
Mountaineering, mountain-walking, rock-climbing,
skiing, mountain rescue.
Week-end, week, and longer; 17 years min. except for
special courses.
Open all year.

MID AND SOUTH WALES

St Christopher's Youth Hostel
Ithen Road, Llandrindod Wells, Radnorshire
Hill-walking.
Week; open to public; 11 years min.
Open all year.

Birch Grove Mountain Centre
Heol Senni, nr. Brecon, Breconshire
Mountaineering, walking, rock-climbing, skiing,
mountain rescue, etc.
Week-end and week; Hampshire Education
Committee users only; 14 years min.
Open all year.

Essex Mountain Centre
Maes y Lade, Velindre, Three Cocks, Breconshire
Mountaineering, walking, skiing, mountain rescue.
Week-end, week, and longer; Essex users only;
14 years min.
Open all year.

Leicester Outdoor Pursuits Centre
Aberglaslyn Hall, Beddgelert, Gwynedd
Mountaineering, walking, rock-climbing, skiing,
mountain rescue.
Week-end, week, and longer; some courses open
to public.
Open all year.

YHA Pen y Pass Hotel
Nant Gwynant, Gwynedd
Mountaineering, walking, rock-climbing.
Week; open to public; 16 years min.
Open all year.

Anglesey Outdoor Education Centre
Beaumaris, Anglesey
Hill-walking.
Week-end and week; Anglesey schools and youth
only; 8 years min.
Open all year.

Coventry Outdoor Pursuits Centre
Plas Dol y Moch, Maentwrog, Merioneth
Mountaineering, walking, rock-climbing.
Week-end, week, 2 weeks; Coventry schools only;
usually 14 years min.
Open all year.

Outward Bound Girls' School
Rhowniar, Tywyn, Merioneth
Mountaineering, walking, rock-climbing,
mountain rescue.
26 days; open to public (ladies only); 16 years min.
Open all year (one mixed course per year).

Plas yr Antur Outdoor Pursuits Centre
Fairbourne, Merioneth
Mountaineering, walking, rock-climbing,
mountain rescue, expedition training.
Week-end and week; open to public and primary and
secondary schools; 11 years min.
Open all year.

Ty'n Berth Mountain Centre
Upper Corris, nr. Machylleth, Gwent
Mountaineering, walking, rock-climbing.
Week; Inner London Education Authority schools
only; 13 years min.
Open all year.

Forest Hill Field Centre
Aberllefenne, nr. Machylleth, Gwent
Mountaineering, walking, field study.
Week-end, week, and longer; not open to public;
12 years min.
Open all year.

The Christian Mountain Centre
Tremadog, Portmadog, Gwynedd
Walking, climbing, canoeing.
Week-end and longer.

Swindon Outdoor Pursuits Centre
Plas Pencelli, Pencelli, Breconshire
Mountaineering, hill-walking, rock-climbing.
Week; open to public; 14 years min.
Open all year.

A Taste of Adventure
Kevin Walker, 18 Gladys Street, Coedely Tonyrefail
Porth, Glamorgan
Mountain-walking, rock-climbing, caving,
mountaineering, navigation, survival.
1, 2, and 5 days; 16 years min. (unless accompanied).
Open all year.

Cecil Lodge
Spa road, Llandrindod Wells, Mid Wales
Pony-trekking, canoeing, rock-climbing, pot-holing,
archery, hill-walking, orienteering, etc.
2 to 7 days.

Dolygaer Outdoor Pursuits Centre
Pontsticill, nr. Merthyr Tydfil, Glamorgan
Mountaineering, walking, rock-climbing,
mountain rescue, caving, orienteering.
Week-end, week, and longer; open to public;
13 years min.
Open all year.

Cardiff Outdoor Pursuits Centre
Nottage, Porthcawl, Glamorgan
Walking, mobile camping.
Week-end, week, and longer; open to Cardiff users only at present; 13 years min.
Open all year.

Abercrave Outdoor Pursuits and Study Centre
Heol Tawe, Abercrave, Swansea
Rock-climbing, hill-walking, caving, canoeing, orienteering, gorge-scrambling, pony-trekking.
Week-end and week; open to public (individuals or groups).
Open all year.

SCOTLAND
County of Lanark Outdoor Pursuits Centre
Airdrie Road, Caldercruix
Walking, rock-climbing.
Week-end and week; open to public; 12 years min.
Open all year.

Glencoe School of Winter Climbing
Tigh Dearg, Glencoe, Argyllshire
Snow- and ice-climbing.
January–April.

Outward Bound Moray
Burghead, Elgin, Moray
Mountaineering, rock-climbing.
26-day Outward Bound Courses; men only; open to public; 14½ years min.

Loch Eil Centre
Achdalieu, Fort William, Inverness-shire
Mountaineering, hill-walking, rock-climbing, mountain rescue.
Week and longer; open to public; 14 years min.
Open all year.

Lagganlia Centre for Outdoor Education
Kincraig, Kingussie, Inverness-shire
Mountaineering, walking, rock-climbing, skiing, field study.
Week-end and week; not open to public.
Open all year.

Glenmore Lodge (Scottish Sports Council)
Aviemore, Inverness-shire
Mountaineering, walking, rock-climbing, skiing, snow- and ice-climbing, mountain rescue, winter survival.
Week and longer; open to public; 17 years min. (except special children's courses).
Open all year.

Benmore Centre for Outdoor Pursuits
Dunoon, Argyllshire
Mountaineering, walking, rock-climbing, mountain rescue.
Week-end, week, and longer; open to Edinburgh schools mainly; no age limit.
Open all year.

John Ridgway School of Adventure
Ardmore, Raiconich, by Lairg, Sutherland
Hill-walking, rock-climbing.
1 and 2 weeks; open to public; 11 years min., 70 years max.
Open April–October.

West Highland School of Adventure
Applecross, Ross-shire
Mountaineering, walking, rock-climbing, mountain rescue.
No short courses; open to public; 14 years min.
Open March–4 December

Glen Brittle Youth Hostel
Glen Brittle, Isle of Skye
Rock-climbing (basic and intermediate).
Week; open to public; 14 years min.
Open July and August.

Climbing on Scotland's West Coast and Island Mountains
Hebridean Holidays Ltd, 2 Upper Dean Street, Edinburgh

Cairngorm Recreation
P O Box 1, Aviemore, Inverness-shire
Mountaincraft, cross-country skiing, rock-climbing, bird-watching, etc.

Sea and Mountain Activities
Peter Cliff, Outdoor Centre, Grantown on Spey
Hill-walking, rock-climbing, canoeing, pony-trekking, orienteering, camping, winter mountaineering, skiing, ski-mountaineering.
Day, week-end, and week for walking, mountaineering, climbing, skiing, and canoeing.

THE SPORTS COUNCIL
70 Brompton Road, London
Several Regional Sports Council offices run day courses at week-ends (details available from Regional Offices).

THE YOUTH HOSTELS ASSOCIATION
Trevelyan House, 8 St Stephen's Hill, St Albans, Herts.
The Scottish Youth Hostels Association,
7 Glebe Crescent, Stirling

Both Associations arrange courses in the British Isles.

169

Youth Hostels

Full details of addresses and information available from The Youth Hostels Association, Trevelyan House, 8 St Stephens Hill, St Albans, Herts AL1 2DY, and The Scottish Youth Hostels Association, 7 Glebe Crescent, Stirling FK8 2JA.

ENGLAND AND WALES
Border and Dales Region
Acomb
Baldersdale
Barnard Castle
Bellingham
Byrness
Durham
Edmundbyers
Greenhead
Grinton Lodge
Keld
Langdon Beck
Newcastle upon Tyne
Ninebanks
Once Brewed
Osmotherley
Rock Hall
Saltburn-by-the-Sea
Westerdale Hall
Whitby
Wooler

Lakeland Region (cont.)
Honister Hause
Kendal
Keswick
Kirkby Stephen
Longthwaite
Patterdale
Slaidburn
Thirlmere
Wastwater
Windermere

Yorkshire Region
Aysgarth Falls
Boggle Hole
Dacre Banks
Dentdale
Earby
Ellingstring
Garsdale Head
Hawes
Haworth

Lakeland Region
Alston
Ambleside
Arnside
Black Sail
Buttermere
Carlisle
Carrock Fell
Cockermouth
Coniston Coppermines
Coniston
Derwentwater
Duddon
Dufton
Elterwater
Ennerdale
Eskdale
Grasmere (Butharlyp How)
Grasmere (Thorney How)
Hawkshead
Helvellyn
High Close

Helmsley
Hull
Ingleton
Kettlewell
Linton
Lockton
Malham
Malton
Mankinholes Hall
Marsden
Ramsgill
Scarborough
Selby
Stainforth
Thixendale
Wheeldale
York

Peak Region
Bakewell
Bretton
Buxton

Peak Region (cont.)
Castleton
Copt Oak
Crowden-in-Longdendale
Dimmingsdale
Edale
Elton
Eyam
Gradbach Mill
Grantham
Hartington
Hathersage
Ilam Hall
Langsett
Lincoln
Matlock Bath
Meerbrook
Ravenstor
Shining Cliff
Thurlby
Windgather Cottage
Woody's Top
Youlgrave
Hagg Farm

North Wales
Bangor
Bryn Gwynant
Capel Curig
Chester
Colwyn Bay
Cynwyd
Ffestiniog
Gerddi Bluog
Harlech
Idwal Cottage
Llanbedr
Llanberis
Llangollen
Lledr Valley
Maeshafn
Oaklands (Betws-y-Coed)
Penmaenmawr
Pen-y-Pass
Plas Rhiwaedog
Ro Wen
Snowdon Ranger

South Wales
Blaencaron
Borth
Broad Haven
Bryn Poeth Uchaf
Capel-y-Ffin
Chepstow
Corris
Crickhowell
Dinas Mawddwy
Dolgoch
Glascwm
Kings (Dolgellau)
Knighton
Llanddeusant
Llwyn-y-Celyn
Marloes Sands
Mitcheldean
Monmouth
Nant-y-Dernol
New Quay
Pentlepoir
Poppit Sands
Port Eynon
Pwll Deri
St Athan
St Briavels Castle
St David's
Trevine
Tyncornel
Ty'n-y-Caeau
Welsh Bicknor
Ystradfellte
Ystumtuen

Midland Region
Badby
Bridges
Charlbury
Cleeve Hill
Clun Mill
Duntisbourne Abbots
Greens Norton
Inglesham
Ironbridge Gorge
Ludlow
Malvern Hills
Oxford
Shrewsbury

Midland Region (cont.)
Slimbridge
Staunton-on-Wye
Stow-on-the-Wold
Stratford-upon-Avon
Wheathill
Wilderhope Manor

Eastern Region
Alpheton
Blaxhall
Bradenham
Brandon
Cambridge
Castle Hedingham
Colchester
Ely
Epping Forest
Great Stambridge
Great Yarmouth
Harlow
Henley-on-Thames
Hertford
Houghton Mill
Hunstanton
Ivinghoe
Jordans
King's Lynn
Lee Gate
Martham
Milton Keynes
Nedging Tye
Norwich
Saffron Walden
St Albans
Sheringham
Walsingham
Windsor

London
Carter Lane
Earls Court
Hampstead Heath
Highgate
Holland House

Southern Region
Alfriston
Arundel
Beachy Head
Blackboys

Southern Region (cont.)
Burley
Canterbury
Crockham Hill
Dover
Ewhurst Green
Goudhurst
Guestling
Hindhead
Holmbury St Mary
Kemsing
Norleywood
Overton
Patcham
Portsmouth
Southampton
Streatley-on-Thames
Tanners Hatch
Telscombe
Truleigh Hill
Winchester

Isle of Wight
Sandown
Totland Bay
Whitwell

South-west Region
Bath
Beer
Bellever
Bigbury-on-Sea
Boscastle Harbour
Boswinger
Bridport
Bristol
Cheddar
Coverack
Cranborne
Crowcombe Heathfield
Elmscott
Exeter
Exford
Gidleigh
Golant
Hayle
Holford
Ilfracombe
Instow
Land's End

South-west Region (cont.)
Litton Cheney
Lownard
Lynton
Maypool
Minehead
Newquay
Pendennis Castle
Penzance
Perranporth
Plymouth
Salcombe
Salisbury

Start Bay
Steps Bridge
Street
Swanage
Tavistock
Tintagel
Treyarnon Bay
West Lulworth

SCOTLAND
Aberdeen
Achininver
Achmelvich
Ardgartan
Armadale
Aviemore
Ayr
Ballater
Braemar
Broadford
Broadmeadows
Cannich
Carbisdale Castle
Carn Dearg
Coldingham
Craig
Crianlarich
Durness
Edinburgh (Bruntsfield)
Edinburgh (Eglinton)
Falkland
Ferniehirst Castle
Garramore
Garth
Glasgow
Glen Affric
Glenbrittle
Glencoe
Glendevon

SCOTLAND (cont.)
Glendoll
Glenisla
Glen Nevis
Helmsdale
Hoy (and Rackwick)
Inverary
Inverbeg
Inverey
Inverness
John o' Groats (Canisbay)
Kendoon

Killin
Kingussie
Kirkwall
Kirk Yetholm
Kyle
Lerwick
Loch Ard
Loch Lochy
Loch Lomond
Lochmaddy
Loch Morlich
Loch Ness
Loch Ossian
Lochranza
Melrose
Minnigaff
Mochrum
Oban
Papa Westray
Perth
Pitlochry
Raasay
Ratagan
Rowardennan
Snoot
Stirling
Stockinish
Strathpeffer
Stromness
Tighnabruaich
Tobermory
Tomintoul
Tongue
Torridon
Trossachs
Uig
Ullapool
Wanlockhead
Whiting Bay

Useful Addresses

The Backpackers Club, 20 St Michael's Road, Tilehurst, Reading, Berkshire RG3 4RP

British Mountaineering Council, Crawford House, Precinct Centre, Booth Street East, Manchester M13 9RZ

The Camping Club of Great Britain & Ireland Ltd, 11 Grosvenor Place, London SW1W 0EY; Northern England office (Association of Cycle and Lightweight Campers), 22 Holmsley Field Lane, Oulton, Leeds

The Caravan Club, East Grinstead House, East Grinstead, West Sussex RH19 1UA

The Council for the Protection of Rural England, 4 Hobart Place, London SW1W 0HY

The Council for the Protection of Rural Wales, 14 Broad Street, Welshpool, Powys SY21 7SD

The Countryside Commission, John Dower House, Crescent Place, Cheltenham, Gloucestershire GL50 3RA

The Countryside Commission for Scotland, Battleby, Redgorton, Perth, Tayside PH1 3EW

The English Tourist Board, 4 Grosvenor Gardens, London SW1W 0DU

The Forestry Commission, 231 Corstophine Road, Edinburgh EH12 7AT

Her Majesty's Stationery Office, 49 High Holborn, London WC1V 6HB (postal address PO Box 569, London SE1 9NH)

Her Majesty's Stationery Office (Scotland), 13A Castle Street, Edinburgh 2

Her Majesty's Stationery Office (Wales), 41 The Hayes, Cardiff

The National Trust, 42 Queen Anne's Gate, London SW1H 9AS

The National Trust for Scotland, 5 Charlotte Square, Edinburgh EH2 4DU

The Ordnance Survey Department, Romsey Road, Maybush, Southampton SO9 4DH

The Ramblers' Association, 1–5 Wandsworth Road, London SW8 2LJ

The Scottish Tourist Board, 23 Ravelston Terrace, Edinburgh EH4 3EU

The Scottish Youth Hostels Association, 7 Glebe Crescent, Stirling FK8 2JA

The Wales Tourist Board, Brunel House, 2 Fitzalan Road, Cardiff CF2 1UY

The Youth Hostels Association, Trevelyan House, 8 St Stephen's Hill, St Albans, Hertfordshire AL1 2DY

Bibliography

R. Clark and E.C. Pyatt, *Mountaineering in Britain*, Phoenix

F. Monkhouse and J. Williams, *Climber and Fell Walker in Lakeland*, David & Charles

A. Clarke and I. Price, *Start Rock Climbing*, Stanley Paul & Co.

M. Marriott, *Start Backpacking*, Stanley Paul & Co.

J. Cleare and R. Collomb, *Sea Cliff Climbing in Britain*, Constable

R. Adshead and D. Booth, *Backpacking in Britain*, Oxford Press

S. Styles, *Backpacking in Wales*, Robert Hale

A. Rowland, *Hillwalking in Snowdonia*, Circerone Press

J. Hillaby, *Journey through Britain*, Granada

The Lake District National Park, Her Majesty's Stationery Office

Peak District National Park, Her Majesty's Stationery Office

North York Moors National Park, Her Majesty's Stationery Office

D.G. Moir, *Scottish Hill Tracks*, John Bartholomew

Snowdonia National Park, Her Majesty's Stationery Office

T. Brown and R. Hunter, *Spur Book of Map and Compass*, Spurbooks

D.A. Robson, *The Science of Geology*, Blandford Press

A. Leutscher, *A Field Guide to the British Countryside*, New English Library

R. Stirling, *The Weather of Britain*, Faber

M. Marriott, *The Footpaths of Britain*, Queen Anne Press

B. Cowley, *The Cleveland Way*, Dalesman Publishing Company

A. Falconer, *The Cleveland Way*, Her Majesty's Stationery Office

C.J. Wright, *The Pilgrims Way and North Downs Way*, Constable

J.B. Jones, *Offa's Dyke Path*, Her Majesty's Stationery Office

F. Noble, *The Shell Book of Offa's Dyke Path*, Queen Anne Press

J.H. Barrett, *The Pembrokeshire Coast Path*, Her Majesty's Stationery Office

T. Stephenson, *The Pennine Way*, Her Majesty's Stationery Office

A. Wainwright, *The Pennine Way Companion*, Westmorland Gazette, Kendal

M. Marriott, *The Shell Book of the Pennine Way*, Queen Anne Press

S. Jennett, *The Ridgeway Path*, Her Majesty's Stationery Office

S. Jennett, *The South Downs Way*, Her Majesty's Stationery Office

E.C. Pyatt, *The Cornwall Coast Path*, Her Majesty's Stationery Office

B. Jackman, *The Dorset Coast Path*, Her Majesty's Stationery Office

M. Marriott, *The Shell Book of the South-West Peninsula Path*, Queen Anne Press

B. Le Mesurier, *The South Devon Coast Path*, Her Majesty's Stationery Office

R. Aitken, *The West Highland Way*, Her Majesty's Stationery Office

Index

Numbers in italics refer to illustrations

INDEX

Acknowledgements
British Tourist Authority: 25 (below), 134, 135, 141, 144, 145, 159
John Cleare. Mountain Camera: 119
J. Allan Cash: 1, 2, 4, 6, 7, 10 (above), 11 (all), 14, 16, 17, 20, 21, 23, 27, 30, 31, 32, 33, 34, 35, 36, 37, 38, 39, 40, 42, 44, 45, 46, 47, 48, 49, 50, 52, 53, 55, 57, 58, 60, 62, 67, 68, 70, 71, 72, 73, 74, 76, 77, 78, 80, 82, 83, 84, 86, 87, 88, 89, 90, 93, 94, 96, 97, 98, 100, 101, 102, 104, 106, 107, 109, 111, 113, 115, 116, 117, 118, 120, 123, 124, 125 (all), 126, 127, 128, 129 (all), 130, 131, 132, 136, 137, 138, 140, 142, 146, 148, 149, 152 (all), 154, 156, 157, 161 (above), 162, 163, 165, 167 (left & centre), 168 (centre & right), 169 (all), 170 (all), 171 (all)
The Lightbox Library: 75
Michael Marriott: 3, 10 (below), 24, 25 (above), 26, 122, 147, 150, 160, 164 (all), 166, 167 (right), 168 (left)
Chris White: 18. 81

The maps were specially commissioned for this book. They were based upon Ordnance Survey maps with the permission of the Controller of Her Majesty's Stationery Office, Crown copyright reserved.

The author and publishers gratefully acknowledge the assistance of West Col Productions, Goring-on-Thames, in supplying information on the climbing areas for use on the maps.

DATE DUE
